HEALTHY CHOICES FOR MEN

100 Days of Devotions

For Mind, Body, and Spirit

Freeman-Smith, LLC.
Nashville, TN 37202

The quoted ideas expressed in this book (but not Scripture verses) are not, in all cases, exact quotations, as some have been edited for clarity and brevity. In all cases, the author has attempted to maintain the speaker's original intent. In some cases, quoted material for this book was obtained from secondary sources, primarily print media. While every effort was made to ensure the accuracy of these sources, the accuracy cannot be guaranteed. For additions, deletions, corrections, or clarifications in future editions of this text, please write Freeman-Smith, LLC.

Cover Design by Kim Russell / Wahoo Designs
Page Layout by Bart Dawson

ISBN 978-1-60587-306-0

Printed in the United States of America

HEALTHY CHOICES FOR MEN

100 Days of Devotions

For Mind, Body, and Spirit

A MESSAGE TO READERS

A wise man will hear and increase learning, and a man of understanding will attain wise counsel.

Proverbs 1:5 NKJV

The advice in this book is general in nature, and your circumstances are specific to you. For that reason, we strongly suggest that you consult your physician before beginning any new regimen of physical exercise or diet. Don't depend upon this book—or any other book like it—to be your sole source of information on matters pertaining to your health. Instead, consider Proverbs 1:5 and seek wise counsel from a variety of sources, especially your personal physician, before making major health-related decisions.

INTRODUCTION

Countless books have been written on the topics of health and fitness. But if you're a Christian, you probably already own at least one copy—and more likely several copies—of the world's foremost guide to spiritual, physical, and emotional fitness. That book is the Holy Bible. The Bible is the irreplaceable guidebook for faithful believers—like you—who seek God's wisdom and His truth.

God has a plan for every aspect of your life, including your food, your fitness, and your faith. But God will not force His plans upon you; to the contrary, He has given you the ability to make choices. The consequences of those choices help determine the quality and the tone of your life. This book is intended to help you make wise choices—choices that will lead to spiritual, physical, and emotional health—by encouraging you to rely heavily upon the promises of God's Holy Word.

Health is a gift from God. What we do with that gift is determined, to a surprising extent, by the person we see every time we gaze into the mirror. If we squander our health—or if we take it for granted—we do a profound disservice to ourselves and to our loved ones. But God has other plans. He commands us to treat our bodies, our minds, and our souls with the utmost care. And that's exactly what we should do.

If you seek to protect and to enhance your spiritual, emotional, and physical health, these pages will help, but they offer no shortcuts. Healthy living is a journey, not a destination, and that journey requires discipline. If you're willing to make the step-by-step journey toward improved health, rest assured that God is taking careful note of your progress . . . and He's quietly urging you to take the next step.

DAY 1

100 DAYS TO A NEW AND IMPROVED YOU

A prudent person foresees the danger ahead and takes precautions. The simpleton goes blindly on and suffers the consequences.

Proverbs 27:12 NLT

It takes time to change a habit, but it doesn't take forever. In fact, if you can do anything for 100 straight days, then there's a very good chance you can keep doing it on the 101st, the 102nd, and beyond. If you thought that you could establish a number of healthy habits, would you be willing to carve out a few minutes each day for the next few months in order to find out? If you answered yes, congratulations. You are about to embark on a grand adventure.

When you form a deeper relationship with God, you can start establishing healthier habits, starting now.

This book contains 100 chapters, each of which contains a devotional message about your mind, your body, and your spirit. If you read each devotional carefully—and if you implement the ideas that you find there—you can have a profound impact on your own life and upon the lives of your loved ones.

FOOD FOR THOUGHT

You can build up a set of good habits so that you habitually take the Christian way without thought.

E. Stanley Jones

You will never change your life until you change something you do daily.

John Maxwell

Since behaviors become habits, make them work with you and not against you.

E. Stanley Jones

Begin to be now what you will be hereafter.

St. Jerome

A HEALTHY-CHOICE TIP

Before you begin a major new exercise program, see your doctor: As the old saying goes, it's better to be safe than sorry.

DAY 2

FORMING HEALTHY HABITS

Dear friend, I pray that you may prosper in every way and be in good health, just as your soul prospers.

3 John 1:2 HCSB

It's an old saying and a true one: First, you make your habits, and then your habits make you. Some habits will inevitably bring you closer to God; other habits will lead you away from the path He has chosen for you. If you sincerely desire to improve your spiritual health, you must honestly examine the habits that make up the fabric of your day. And you must abandon those habits that are displeasing to God.

If you trust God, and if you keep asking for His help, He can transform your life. If you sincerely ask Him to help you, the same God who created the universe will help you defeat the harmful habits that have heretofore defeated you. So, if at first you don't succeed, keep praying. God is listening, and He's ready to help you become a better person if you ask Him . . . so ask today.

Today, ask God to help you form healthier habits. If you ask for His help—if you petition Him sincerely and often—your Heavenly Father will guide your steps and protect you from harmful behaviors.

FOOD FOR THOUGHT

We are never out of reach of Satan's devices, so we must never be without the whole armor of God.

Warren Wiersbe

Acquire wisdom—how much better it is than gold! And acquire understanding—it is preferable to silver.

Proverbs 16:16 HCSB

If you want to form a new habit, get to work. If you want to break a bad habit, get on your knees.

Marie T. Freeman

A HEALTHY-CHOICE TIP

Do you dine out often? If so, be careful. Most restaurants stay in business by serving big portions of tasty food. Unfortunately, most restaurant food is high in calories, sugar, and fat. You will probably eat healthier meals if you prepare those meals at home instead of eating out.

DAY 3

RESPECTING YOUR BODY

Therefore, brothers, by the mercies of God, I urge you to present your bodies as a living sacrifice, holy and pleasing to God; this is your spiritual worship.

Romans 12:1 HCSB

In the 12th chapter of Romans, Paul encourages us to take special care of the bodies God has given us. But it's tempting to do otherwise.

We live in a fast-food world where unhealthy choices are convenient, inexpensive, and tempting. And, we live in a digital world filled with modern conveniences that often rob us of the physical exercise needed to maintain healthy lifestyles. As a result, too many of us find ourselves glued to the television, with a snack in one hand and a clicker in the other. The results are as unfortunate as they are predictable.

If you're not determined to be the master of your body . . . then you might just become a slave to your impulses.

God's Word teaches us that our bodies are "temples" that belong to God (1 Corinthians 6:19-20). We are commanded (not encouraged, not advised—we are commanded!) to treat our bodies with respect and honor. We do so by making wise choices and by making those choices consistently: day by day, month by month, and year by year.

FOOD FOR THOUGHT

Food ought to be a refreshment to the body, and not a burden.

St. Bonaventure

Eat to live, and not live to eat.

Poor Richard's Almanac

For it was You who created my inward parts; You knit me together in my mother's womb. I will praise You, because I have been remarkably and wonderfully made.

Psalm 139:13-14 HCSB

A HEALTHY-CHOICE TIP

Take a few minutes to examine your eating habits. Do you gobble down snack foods while watching television? If so, stop. Do you drink high-calorie soft drinks or feast on unhealthy snacks like potato chips or candy? If so, you're doing yourself a disservice. Do you load up your plate and then feel obligated to eat every last bite? If so, it's time to form some new habits.

Poor eating habits are usually well established, so they won't be easy to change, but change them you must if you want to enjoy the benefits of a healthy lifestyle.

DAY 4

YOUR PARTNERSHIP WITH GOD

So now we can rejoice in our wonderful new relationship with God—all because of what our Lord Jesus Christ has done for us in making us friends of God.

Romans 5:11 NLT

If you're like most men, you've already tried, perhaps on many occasions, to form healthier habits. You've employed your own willpower in a noble effort to create a new, improved, healthier you. You've probably tried to improve various aspects of your spiritual, physical, or emotional health. Perhaps you've gone on diets, or made New Year's resolutions, or tried the latest self-help fad in an attempt to finally make important changes in your life. And if you're like most men, you've been successful . . . for a while. But eventually, those old familiar habits came creeping back into your life, and the improvements that you had made proved to be temporary. This book is intended to help you build a series of healthy habits for your Christian walk . . . and make those habits stick.

Your journey toward improved health can be, and should be, a journey that you make with God.

As you read through the pages of this book, you will be asked to depend less upon your own willpower and more upon God's power. For 100 days, you'll be asked to focus on three major areas of your life: diet, fitness, and faith. And, of this you can be sure: When you form a working relationship with the Creator, there's no limit to the things that the two of you, working together, can do in just 100 days.

FOOD FOR THOUGHT

Faith is not merely you holding on to God—it is God holding on to you.

E. Stanley Jones

He stands fast as your rock, steadfast as your safeguard, sleepless as your watcher, valiant as your champion.

C. H. Spurgeon

A HEALTHY-CHOICE TIP

Perhaps you have tended to divide the concerns of your life into two categories: "spiritual" and "other." If so, it's time to reconsider. God intends for you to integrate His commandments into every aspect of your life, and that includes your physical and emotional health, too.

DAY 5

FAITH AND FITNESS

Cast your burden on the Lord, and He shall sustain you; He shall never permit the righteous to be moved.

Psalm 55:22 NKJV

Faith and fitness. These two words may seem disconnected, but they are not. If you're about to begin a regimen of vigorous physical exercise, then you will find it helpful to begin a regimen of vigorous spiritual exercise, too. Why? Because the physical, emotional, and spiritual aspects of your life are interconnected. In other words, you cannot "compartmentalize" physical fitness in one category of your being and spiritual fitness in another—every facet of your life has an impact on the person you are today and the person you will become tomorrow. That's why your body is so important to God—your body is, quite literally, the "temple" that houses "the Spirit of God" that dwells within you (1 Corinthians 3:16).

Today, spend time thinking about God's plans for your spiritual and physical health.

God's Word contains powerful lessons about every aspect of your life, including your health. So, if you're concerned about your spiritual, physical, or emotional health, the first place to turn is that timeless source of comfort and assurance, the Holy Bible. When you open your Bible and begin reading, you'll quickly be reminded of this fact: when you face concerns of any sort—including health-related challenges—God is with you. And His healing touch, like His love, endures forever.

FOOD FOR THOUGHT

Only by walking with God can we hope to find the path that leads to life.

John Eldredge

God surrounds you with opportunity. You and I are free in Jesus Christ, not to do whatever we want, but to be all that God wants us to be.

Warren Wiersbe

STRENGTHENING YOUR FAITH

God has given us the Bible for the purpose of knowing His promises, His power, His commandments, His wisdom, His love, and His Son. As we study God's teachings and apply them to our lives, we live by the Word that shall never pass away. So if you're about to begin a new fitness program, be sure that you also pay careful attention to God's program by studying His Word every day of your life.

DAY 6

PUTTING GOD FIRST

But seek first the kingdom of God and His righteousness, and all these things will be provided for you.

Matthew 6:33 HCSB

One of the quickest ways to accomplish any worthy goal—perhaps the only way—is to do it with God as your partner. So here's a question worth thinking about: Have you made God your top priority by offering Him your heart, your soul, your talents, and your time? Or are you in the habit of giving God little more than a few hours on Sunday morning? The answer to these questions will determine, to a surprising extent, the direction of your day and the condition of your character.

Are you really putting God first in your life, or are you putting other things—like possessions, pleasures, or personal status—ahead of your relationship with Him?

As you contemplate your own relationship with God, remember this: all of mankind is engaged in the practice of worship. Some folks choose to worship God and, as a result, reap the joy that He intends for His children to experience. Other folks, folks who are stubbornly determined to do it "their way," distance themselves from God by worshiping such things as earthly possessions or personal gratification . . . and when they do, they suffer.

In the book of Exodus, God warns that we should place no gods before Him (20:3). Yet all too often, we place our Lord in second, third, or fourth place as we worship the gods of pride, greed, power, or lust.

Does God rule your heart? Make certain that the honest answer to this question is a resounding yes. If you sincerely wish to build your character and your life on an unshakable foundation, you must put your Creator in first place. No exceptions.

FOOD FOR THOUGHT

We become whatever we are committed to.

Rick Warren

God calls us to be committed to Him, to be committed to making a difference, and to be committed to reconciliation.

Bill Hybels

STRENGTHENING YOUR FAITH

As you establish priorities for your day and your life, God deserves first place. And you deserve the experience of putting Him there.

DAY 7

DON'T GO ON A DIET, CHANGE YOUR LIFESTYLE

Their end is destruction; their god is their stomach; their glory is in their shame. They are focused on earthly things.

Philippians 3:19 HCSB

If you want to lose weight, don't dare go on a diet! It's a sad fact, but true: in the vast majority of cases, diets simply don't work. In fact, one study that examined the results of popular diets conducted that nearly 100% of dieters suffered almost "complete relapse after 3 to 5 years." In other words, dieters almost always return to their pre-diet weights (or, in many cases, to even higher weight levels).

If diets don't work, what should you do if you weigh more than you should? The answer is straightforward: If you need to lose weight, don't start dieting; change your lifestyle.

It takes wisdom to be moderate; moderation is wisdom in action.

Your current weight is the result of the number of calories that you have taken into your body versus the number of calories that you have burned. If you seek to lower your weight, then you must burn more calories (by engaging in more vigorous physical activities), or take in fewer calories (by eating more sensibly), or both. It's as simple as that.

FOOD FOR THOUGHT

It's not that some people have willpower and some don't. It's that some people are ready to change and others are not.

James Gordon, M.D.

You can look at your calorie count in the same way you might look at a bank account. Every mouthful of food is a deposit and every activity that requires energy is a withdrawal. If we deposit more than we withdraw, our surplus grows larger and larger.

John Maxwell

We are all created differently. We share a common need to balance the different parts of our lives.

Dr. Walt Larimore

To many, total abstinence is easier than perfect moderation.

St. Augustine

A HEALTHY-CHOICE TIP

Are you skipping meals? Don't do it. Skipping meals isn't healthy, and it isn't a sensible way to lose weight, either.

DAY 8

IT ALL STARTS WITH GOD

Now the God of all grace, who called you to His eternal glory in Christ Jesus, will personally restore, establish, strengthen, and support you.

1 Peter 5:10 HCSB

Physical fitness, like every other aspect of your life, begins and ends with God. If you'd like to adopt a healthier lifestyle, God is willing to help. In fact, if you sincerely wish to create a healthier you—either physically, emotionally or spiritually—God is anxious to be your silent partner in that endeavor, but it's up to you to ask for His help.

Today, think about the ways that your spiritual, emotional, and physical health are interconnected.

The journey toward improved health is not only a common-sense exercise in personal discipline, it is also a spiritual journey ordained by our Creator. God does not intend that we abuse our bodies by giving in to excessive appetites or to slothful behavior. To the contrary, God has instructed us to protect our physical bodies to the greatest extent we can. To do otherwise is to disobey Him.

God has a plan for every facet of your life, and His plan includes provisions for your spiritual, physical, and emotional health. But, He expects you to do your fair share of the work! In a world that is chock-full of tasty temptations, you may find it all too easy to make unhealthy choices. Your challenge, of course, is to resist those unhealthy choices by every means you can, including prayer. And you can be sure that whenever you ask for God's help, He will give it.

FOOD FOR THOUGHT

He goes before us, follows behind us, and hems us safe inside the realm of His protection.

Beth Moore

Prayer is our pathway not only to divine protection, but also to a personal, intimate relationship with God.

Shirley Dobson

STRENGTHENING YOUR FAITH

Ruth Bell Graham, wife of evangelist Billy Graham, observed: "The Reference Point for the Christian is the Bible. All values, judgments, and attitudes must be gauged in relationship to this Reference Point." Make certain that you're an avid reader of God's best-seller, and make sure that you keep reading it as long as you live!

DAY 9

SAY NO TO UNHEALTHY FOODS

Dear friend, I pray that you may prosper in every way and be in good health, just as your soul prospers.

3 John 1:2 HCSB

Eating unhealthy foods is habit-forming. And if you have acquired the unfortunate habit of eating unhealthy foods, then God wants you start making changes today.

Take a few more minutes than you did on day 3 to think about your eating habits. Are you really ready to improve your diet, your health, and your life?

Poor eating habits are easy to make and hard to break, but break them you must. Otherwise, you'll be disobeying God's commandments while causing yourself great harm.

Today, think about some of the foods that you should eliminate from your diet.

Maintaining a healthy lifestyle is a journey, not a destination, and that journey requires discipline. But rest assured that if you and your loved ones are willing to make the step-by-step journey toward a healthier diet, God is taking careful note of your progress . . . and He's quietly urging you to take the next step.

FOOD FOR THOUGHT

The man who prays ceases to be a fool.

Oswald Chambers

Virtue—even attempted virtue—brings light; indulgence brings fog.

C. S. Lewis

Wisdom takes us beyond the realm of mere right and wrong. Wisdom takes into account our personalities, our strengths, our weaknesses, and even our present state of mind.

Charles Stanley

In general, mankind, since the improvement of cookery, eats twice as much as nature requires.

Ben Franklin

A HEALTHY-CHOICE TIP

Adopt healthy habits you can stick with. In other words, don't starve yourself. And if you're beginning an exercise regimen, start slowly. Be moderate, even in your moderation.

DAY 10

HAVE A REGULAR APPOINTMENT WITH GOD

He awakens Me morning by morning, He awakens My ear to hear as the learned. The Lord God has opened My ear.

Isaiah 50:4-5 NKJV

Do you have a strength-building, life-altering, standing appointment with God every morning? Is God your first priority, or do talk with Him less frequently than that? If you're wise, you'll talk to God first thing every day, without exception.

Warren Wiersbe writes, "Surrender your mind to the Lord at the beginning of each day." And that's sound advice. When you begin each day with your head bowed and your heart lifted, you are reminded of God's love, His protection, and His commandments. Then, you can align your priorities for the coming day with the teachings and commandments that God has placed upon your heart.

Would you like a foolproof formula for a better life? Here it is: stay in close contact with the Father.

Each day has 1,440 minutes—can you give God a few of them? Of course you can . . . and of course you should. So if you've acquired the unfortunate habit of trying to "squeeze" God into the corners of your life, it's time to reshuffle the items on your to-do list by placing God first. And if you haven't already done so, form the habit of spending quality time each morning with your Creator. He deserves it . . . and so, for that matter, do you.

FOOD FOR THOUGHT

We must appropriate the tender mercy of God every day after conversion or problems quickly develop. We need his grace daily in order to live a righteous life.

Jim Cymbala

I suggest you discipline yourself to spend time daily in a systematic reading of God's Word. Make this "quiet time" a priority that nobody can change.

Warren Wiersbe

STRENGTHENING YOUR FAITH

Make a promise to yourself and keep it that you will begin each day with a morning devotional. A regular time of quiet reflection and prayer will allow you to praise your Creator and to focus your thoughts. A daily devotional is especially important during those times of your life when you're feeling discouraged or fearful.

DAY 11

IF NOT NOW, WHEN?

Therefore, get your minds ready for action, being self-disciplined, and set your hope completely on the grace to be brought to you at the revelation of Jesus Christ.

1 Peter 1:13 HCSB

If you're determined to improve the state of your physical, spiritual, or emotional health, the best time to begin is now. But if you're like most people, you'll be tempted to put things off until tomorrow, or the next day, or the next.

The habit of putting things off until the last minute, along with its first cousin, the habit of making excuses for work that was never done, can be detrimental to your life, to your character, and to your health. Are you in the habit of doing what needs to be done when it needs to be done, or are you a dues-paying member of the Procrastinator's Club? If you're a man who has already acquired the habit of doing things sooner rather than later, congratulations! But, if you find yourself putting off all those unpleasant tasks until later (or never), it's time to think about the consequences of your behavior.

When it comes to food, fitness, or faith, the best moment to begin major improvements is the present moment.

One way that you can learn to defeat procrastination is by paying less attention to the sacrifices you're making today and more attention to the rewards you'll receive tomorrow. So, if you're trying to improve your fitness, or any other aspect of your life, don't spend endless hours fretting over your fate. Simply seek God's counsel and get busy. When you do, you will be richly rewarded because of your willingness to act.

FOOD FOR THOUGHT

We spend our lives dreaming of the future, not realizing that a little of it slips away every day.

Barbara Johnson

A HEALTHY-CHOICE TIP

Healthy choices are easy to put off until some future date. But procrastination, especially concerning matters of personal health, is, at best, foolish and, at worst, dangerous. If you feel the need to improve your physical health, don't wait for New Year's Day; don't even wait until tomorrow. The time to begin living a healthier life is the moment you finish reading this sentence.

DAY 12

DO FIRST THINGS FIRST

Therefore, get your minds ready for action, being self-disciplined . . . .

1 Peter 1:13 HCSB

"First things first." These words are easy to speak but hard to put into practice. For a busy man living in a demanding world, placing first things first can be difficult indeed. Why? Because so many people are expecting so many things from you!

If you're having trouble prioritizing your day, perhaps you've been trying to organize your life according to your own plans, not God's. A better strategy, of course, is to take your daily obligations and place them in the hands of the One who created you. To do so, you must prioritize your day according to God's commandments, and you must seek His will and His wisdom in all matters. Then, you can face the day with the assurance that the same God who created our universe out of nothingness will help you place first things first in your own life.

Your Heavenly Father wants you to prioritize your day and your life. And the best place to start is by putting God first.

Do you feel overwhelmed or confused? Turn the concerns of this day over to God—prayerfully, earnestly, and often. Then listen for His answer . . . and trust the answer He gives.

FOOD FOR THOUGHT

Sin is largely a matter of mistaken priorities. Any sin in us that is cherished, hidden, and not confessed will cut the nerve center of our faith.

Catherine Marshall

The moment you wake up each morning, all your wishes and hopes for the day rush at you like wild animals. And the first job each morning consists in shoving it all back; in listening to that other voice, taking that other point of view, letting that other, larger, stronger, quieter life coming flowing in.

C. S. Lewis

A HEALTHY-CHOICE TIP

If you're trying to reshape your physique or your life, don't try to do it alone. Ask for the support and encouragement of your family members and friends. You'll improve your odds of success if you enlist your own cheering section.

DAY 13

THE RIGHT KIND OF EXERCISE FOR YOU

He gives strength to the weary and strengthens the powerless.

Isaiah 40:29 HCSB

If you want to attain and maintain a healthy lifestyle, it's important to engage in a consistent exercise program. Implementing a plan of regular, sensible exercise is one way of ensuring that you've done your part to care for the body that God has given you.

Dr. Kenneth Cooper observed, "Physical activity achieved at any level is an essential ingredient in slowing down the process of aging and turning life into a far more useful, enjoyable—and independent—affair." So what's the right kind of exercise for you? That's a question for you and your doctor. But whether you're running marathons or walking around the block, it's important to stay as active as you can, as long as you can.

Your exercise regimen should be sensible, enjoyable, safe, and consistent.

No one can force you to exercise . . . you'll need to make that decision on your own. And if you genuinely desire to please God, it's a decision that you will make today.

FOOD FOR THOUGHT

People who exercise at least 3 hours a week tend to eat a more balanced and a healthier diet.

Dr. Walt Larimore

Give at least two hours every day to exercise, for health must not be sacrificed to learning. A strong body makes the mind strong.

Thomas Jefferson

It is remarkable how one's wits are sharpened by physical exercise.

Pliny the Younger

An early morning walk is a blessing for the whole day.

Henry David Thoreau

A HEALTHY-CHOICE TIP

The benefits of exercise are both both physical and emotional. But no one can exercise for you; it's up to you to exercise, or not.

DAY 14

FOOD MATTERS

Do not carouse with drunkards and gluttons, for they are on their way to poverty.

Proverbs 23:20-21 NLT

Many of us are remarkably ill-informed and amazingly apathetic about the foods we eat. We feast on high-fat fast foods. We swoon over sweets. We order up—and promptly pack away—prodigious portions. The result is a society in which too many of us become the human equivalents of the portions we purchase: oversized.

Today, think carefully about the quality and the quantity of the foods you eat.

A healthier strategy, of course, is to pay more attention to the nutritional properties of our foods and less attention their taste. But for those of us who have become accustomed to large quantities of full-flavored, high-calorie foods, old memories indeed die hard.

Should we count every calorie that we ingest from now until the day the Good Lord calls us home? Probably not. When we focus too intently upon weight reduction, we may make weight loss even harder to achieve. Instead, we should eliminate from our diets the foods that are obviously bad for us and we should eat more of the foods that are obviously good for us. And of course, we should eat sensible amounts, not prodigious portions.

FOOD FOR THOUGHT

Moderation is better than muscle, self-control better than political power.

Proverbs 16:32 MSG

Now the God of all grace, who called you to His eternal glory in Christ Jesus, will personally restore, establish, strengthen, and support you.

1 Peter 5:10 HCSB

Every achievement worth remembering is stained with the blood of diligence and scarred by the wounds of disappointment.

Charles Swindoll

A HEALTHY-CHOICE TIP

Since God loves you, and since He wants the very best for you, don't you believe that He also wants you to enjoy a healthy lifestyle? Of course He does. And since a healthy lifestyle is what God wants for you, isn't it what you should want, too?

DAY 15

SO MANY TEMPTATIONS

Don't you know that you are God's sanctuary and that the Spirit of God lives in you?

1 Corinthians 3:16 HCSB

Our world is teeming with temptations and distractions that can rob you of the physical, emotional, and spiritual fitness that might otherwise be yours. And if you're not careful, the struggles and stresses of everyday living can rob you of the peace that should rightfully be yours because of your personal relationship with Christ.

Take time each day to have a personal training session with your Savior. Don't be a man who's satisfied with occasional visits to church on Sunday morning; build a relationship with Jesus that deepens day by day. When you do, you will most certainly encounter the subtle hand of the Father. Then, if you are wise, you will take His hand and follow God as He leads you on the path to a healthier, happier life.

Think about ways that your spiritual health impacts your physical health, and vice-versa.

FOOD FOR THOUGHT

Most Christians do not know or fully realize that the adversary of our lives is Satan and that his main tool is our flesh, our old nature.

Bill Bright

The first step on the way to victory is to recognize the enemy.

Corrie ten Boom

The Devil is a master strategist. He varies his attacks as skillfully as an experienced general and always has one more trick to use against the one who imagines he is well experienced in the holy war.

A. W. Tozer

You have to say "yes" to God first before you can effectively say "no" to the devil.

Vance Havner

A HEALTHY-CHOICE TIP

If life's inevitable temptations seem to be getting the best of you, try praying more often, even if many of those prayers are simply brief, "open-eyed" requests to your Father in heaven.

DAY 16

GUARD YOUR HEART AND MIND

Finally, brethren, whatever things are true, whatever things are noble, whatever things are just, whatever things are pure, whatever things are lovely, whatever things are of good report, if there is any virtue and if there is anything praiseworthy—meditate on these things.

Philippians 4:8 NKJV

You are near and dear to God. He loves you more than you can imagine, and He wants the very best for you. And one more thing: God wants you to guard your heart.

Every day, you are faced with choices . . . more choices than you can count. You can do the right thing, or not. You can be prudent, or not. You can be kind, and generous, and obedient to God. Or not.

Today, think about ways that you can guard your heart from temptation and stress.

Today, the world will offer you countless opportunities to let down your guard and, by doing so, make needless mistakes that may injure you or your loved ones. So be watchful and obedient. Guard your heart by giving it to your Heavenly Father; it is safe with Him.

FOOD FOR THOUGHT

He doesn't need an abundance of words. He doesn't need a dissertation about your life. He just wants your attention. He wants your heart.

Kathy Troccoli

If all struggles and sufferings were eliminated, the spirit would no more reach maturity than would the child.

Elisabeth Elliot

Be sober! Be on the alert! Your adversary the Devil is prowling around like a roaring lion, looking for anyone he can devour.

1 Peter 5:8 HCSB

How little people know who think that holiness is dull. When one meets the real thing, it's irresistible.

C. S. Lewis

STRENGTHENING YOUR FAITH

You should do whatever it takes to guard your heart—and with God's help, you can do it.

DAY 17

MOVING MOUNTAINS

If you have faith as a mustard seed, you will say to this mountain, "Move from here to there," and it will move; and nothing will be impossible for you.

Matthew 17:20 NKJV

Every life—including yours—is a series of successes and failures, celebrations and disappointments, joys and sorrows. Every step of the way, through every triumph and tragedy, God will stand by your side and strengthen you . . . if you have faith in Him. Jesus taught His disciples that if they had faith, they could move mountains. You can, too.

Prayer changes things—and you—so pray.

When a suffering woman sought healing by merely touching the hem of His cloak, Jesus replied, "Daughter, be of good comfort; thy faith hath made thee whole" (Matthew 9:22 KJV). The message to believers of every generation is clear: we must live by faith today and every day.

When you place your faith, your trust, indeed your life in the hands of Christ Jesus, you'll be amazed at the marvelous things He can do with you and through you. So strengthen your faith through praise, through worship, through Bible study, and through prayer. And trust God's plans. With Him, all things are possible, and He stands ready to open a world of possibilities to you . . . if you have faith.

FOOD FOR THOUGHT

There are a lot of things in life that are difficult to understand. Faith allows the soul to go beyond what the eyes can see.

John Maxwell

The popular idea of faith is of a certain obstinate optimism: the hope, tenaciously held in the face of trouble, that the universe is fundamentally friendly and things may get better.

J. I. Packer

When you enroll in the "school of faith," you never know what may happen next. The life of faith presents challenges that keep you going—and keep you growing!

Warren Wiersbe

STRENGTHENING YOUR FAITH

The quality of your faith will help determine the quality of your day and the quality of your life.

DAY 18

BEYOND BITTERNESS

All bitterness, anger and wrath, insult and slander must be removed from you, along with all wickedness. And be kind and compassionate to one another, forgiving one another, just as God also forgave you in Christ.

Ephesians 4:31-32 HCSB

Bitterness is a stress-inducing spiritual sickness. It will consume your soul; it is dangerous to your emotional health. It can destroy you if you let it . . . so don't let it!

Today, make a list of the people you need to forgive and the things you need to forget.

If you are caught up in intense feelings of anger or resentment, you know all too well the destructive power of these emotions. How can you rid yourself of these feelings? First, you must prayerfully ask God to cleanse your heart. Then, you must learn to catch yourself whenever thoughts of bitterness or hatred begin to attack you. Your challenge is this: You must learn to resist negative thoughts before they hijack your emotions.

The Bible teaches us that if we judge our brothers and sisters, we, too, will be subject to judgment. Let us refrain, then, from judging our neighbors. Instead, let us forgive them and love them, while leaving their judgment to a far more capable authority: the One who sits on His throne in heaven.

FOOD FOR THOUGHT

Bitterness only makes suffering worse and closes the spiritual channels through which God can pour His grace.

Warren Wiersbe

Bitterness is the greatest barrier to friendship with God.

Rick Warren

Be patient and understanding. Life is too short to be vengeful or malicious.

Phillips Brooks

Bitterness is the trap that snares the hunter.

Max Lucado

A HEALTHY-CHOICE TIP

Holding a grudge? Drop it! Remember, holding a grudge is like letting somebody live rent-free in your brain . . . so don't do it!

DAY 19

RICHLY BLESSED

The Lord bless you and keep you; the Lord make His face shine upon you, and be gracious to you.

Numbers 6:24-25 NKJV

Because we have been so richly blessed, we should make thanksgiving a habit, a regular part of our daily routines. But sometimes, amid the stresses and obligations of everyday life, we may allow interruptions and distractions to interfere with the time we spend with God.

If you need a little cheering up, start counting your blessings. In truth, you really have too many blessings to count, but it never hurts to try.

Have you counted your blessings today? And have you thanked God for them? Hopefully so. After all, God's gifts include your family, your friends, your talents, your opportunities, your possessions, and the priceless gift of eternal life. How glorious are these gifts . . . and God is responsible for every one of them.

So today, as you go about the duties of everyday life, pause and give thanks to the Creator. He deserves your praise, and you deserve the experience of praising Him.

FOOD FOR THOUGHT

God's kindness is not like the sunset—brilliant in its intensity, but dying every second. God's generosity keeps coming and coming and coming.

Bill Hybels

Do we not continually pass by blessings innumerable without notice, and instead fix our eyes on what we feel to be our trials and our losses, and think and talk about these until our whole horizon is filled with them, and we almost begin to think we have no blessings at all?

Hannah Whitall Smith

God is more anxious to bestow His blessings on us than we are to receive them.

St. Augustine

God blesses us in spite of our lives and not because of our lives.

Max Lucado

STRENGTHENING YOUR FAITH

God gives each of us countless blessings. We, in turn, should give Him our thanks and our praise. So remember: the best moment to give thanks is always the present moment.

DAY 20

TOO BUSY?

Careful planning puts you ahead in the long run; hurry and scurry puts you further behind.

Proverbs 21:5 MSG

Are you making time each day to praise God and to study His Word? If so, you know firsthand the blessings that He offers those who worship Him consistently and sincerely. But, if you have unintentionally allowed the hustle and bustle of your busy day to come between you and your Creator, then you must slow down, take a deep breath, and rearrange your priorities.

God loved this world so much that He sent His Son to save it. And now only one real question remains for you: what will you do in response to God's love? The answer should be obvious: God must come first in your life. He is the giver of all good things, and He is the One who sent His Son so that you might have eternal life. He deserves your prayers, your obedience, your stewardship, and your love—and He deserves these things all day every day, not just on Sunday mornings.

Do first things first, and keep your focus on high-priority tasks. And remember this: your highest priority should be your relationship with God and His Son.

FOOD FOR THOUGHT

How busy we have become . . . and as a result, how empty!

Charles Swindoll

The foe of opportunity is preoccupation. Just when God sends along a chance to turn a great victory for mankind, some of us are too busy puttering around to notice it.

A. W. Tozer

We often become mentally and spiritually barren because we're so busy.

Franklin Graham

The most powerful life is the most simple life. The most powerful life is the life that knows where it's going, that knows where the source of strength is; it is the life that stays free of clutter and happenstance and hurriedness.

Max Lucado

STRENGTHENING YOUR FAITH

The world wants to grab every spare minute of your time, but God wants some of your time, too. When in doubt, trust God.

DAY 21

MODERATION LEADS TO ABUNDANCE

Don't associate with those who drink too much wine, or with those who gorge themselves on meat. For the drunkard and the glutton will become poor, and grogginess will clothe [them] in rags.

Proverbs 23:20-21 HCSB

If you sincerely seek the abundant life that Christ has promised, you must learn to control your appetites before they control you. Good habits, like bad ones, are habit-forming. The sooner you acquire the habit of moderation, the better your chances for a long, happy, abundant life.

Today, think of at least one step you can take to become a more moderate person.

Are you running short on willpower? If so, perhaps you haven't yet asked God to give you strength. The Bible promises that God offers His power to those righteous men and women who earnestly seek it. If your willpower has failed you on numerous occasions, then it's time to turn your weaknesses over to God. If you've been having trouble standing on your own two feet, perhaps it's time to drop to your knees, in prayer.

FOOD FOR THOUGHT

God wants to revolutionize our lives—by showing us how knowing Him can be the most powerful force to help us become all we want to be.

Bill Hybels

Believe and do what God says. The life-changing consequences will be limitless, and the results will be confidence and peace of mind.

Franklin Graham

Peace, peace to you, and peace to your helpers! For your God *helps you.*

1 Chronicles 12:18 NKJV

A HEALTHY-CHOICE TIP

Life is a gift—health must be earned. We earn good health by cultivating healthy habits. This is the right time for you to commit yourself to a more sensible lifestyle. So take a close look at your habits: how you eat, how you exercise, and how you think about your health. The only way that you'll revolutionize your physical health is to revolutionize the habits that make up the fabric of your day.

DAY 22

LISTENING TO GOD

The one who is from God listens to God's words. This is why you don't listen, because you are not from God.

John 8:47 HCSB

Sometimes God speaks loudly and clearly. More often, He speaks in a quiet voice—and if you are wise, you will be listening carefully when He does. To do so, you must carve out quiet moments each day to study His Word and sense His direction.

Can you quiet yourself long enough to listen to your conscience? Are you attuned to the subtle guidance of your intuition? Are you willing to pray sincerely and then to wait quietly for God's response? Hopefully so. Usually God refrains from sending His messages on stone tablets or city billboards. More often, He communicates in subtler ways. If you sincerely desire to hear His voice, you must listen carefully, and you must do so in the silent corners of your quiet, willing heart.

Today, find time to be quiet and still. Then, in the silence, listen carefully to your Creator.

FOOD FOR THOUGHT

The first service one owes to others in the fellowship consists in listening to them. Just as love of God begins in listening to His Word, so the beginning of love for the brethren is learning to listen to them.

Dietrich Bonhoeffer

The center of power is not to be found in summit meetings or in peace conferences. It is not in Peking or Washington or the United Nations, but rather where a child of God prays in the power of the Spirit for God's will to be done in her life, in her home, and in the world around her.

Ruth Bell Graham

In the soul-searching of our lives, we are to stay quiet so we can hear Him say all that He wants to say to us in our hearts.

Charles Swindoll

STRENGTHENING YOUR FAITH

God is trying to get your attention. Are you listening?

DAY 23

IT TAKES DISCIPLINE

Apply your heart to discipline and your ears to words of knowledge.

Proverbs 23:12 NASB

Today, think about the costs and the benefits of discipline.

Physical fitness requires discipline: the discipline to exercise regularly and the discipline to eat sensibly—it's as simple as that. But here's the catch: understanding the need for discipline is easy, but leading a disciplined life can be hard for most of us. Why? Because it's usually more fun to eat a second piece of cake than it is to jog a second lap around the track. But, as we survey the second helpings that all too often find their way on to our plates, we should consider this: as Christians, we are instructed to lead disciplined lives, and when we behave in undisciplined ways, we are living outside God's will.

God's Word reminds us again and again that our Creator expects us to be disciplined in our thoughts and disciplined in our actions. God doesn't reward laziness, misbehavior, apathy, or shortsightedness. To the contrary, He expects believers to behave with dignity and self-control.

We live in a world in which leisure is glorified and consumption is commercialized. But God has other plans.

He did not create us for lives of gluttony of sloth; He created us for far greater things.

Life's greatest rewards seldom fall into our laps; to the contrary, our greatest accomplishments usually require lots of work, which is perfectly fine with God. After all, He knows that we're up to the task, and He has big plans for us; may we, as disciplined believers, always be worthy of those plans.

FOOD FOR THOUGHT

I discipline my body and bring it under strict control, so that after preaching to others, I myself will not be disqualified.

1 Corinthians 9:27 HCSB

Discipline is training that develops and corrects.

Charles Stanley

Work is doing it. Discipline is doing it every day. Diligence is doing it well every day.

Dave Ramsey

A HEALTHY-CHOICE TIP

Discipline matters. It takes discipline to strengthen your faith; it takes discipline to improve your fitness.

DAY 24

ADVERSITY BUILDS CHARACTER

God is our refuge and strength, a very present help in trouble.

Psalm 46:1 NKJV

As life here on earth unfolds, all of us encounter occasional disappointments and setbacks: Those occasional visits from Old Man Trouble are simply a fact of life, and none of us are exempt. When tough times arrive, we may be forced to rearrange our plans and our priorities. But even on our darkest days, we must remember that God's love remains constant. And we must never forget that God intends for us to use our setbacks as stepping stones on the path to a better life.

If you're having tough times, don't hit the panic button and don't keep everything bottled up inside. Talk things over with people you can really trust.

The fact that we encounter adversity is not nearly so important as the way we choose to deal with it. When tough times arrive, we have a clear choice: we can begin the difficult work of tackling our troubles . . . or not. When we summon the courage to look Old Man Trouble squarely in the eye, he usually blinks. But, if we refuse to address our problems, even the smallest annoyances have a way of growing into king-sized catastrophes.

Psalm 145 promises, "The Lord is near to all who call on him, to all who call on him in truth. He fulfills the desires of those who fear him; he hears their cry and saves them" (vv. 18-20 NIV). And the words of Jesus offer us comfort: "These things I have spoken to you, that in Me you may have peace. In the world you will have tribulation; but be of good cheer, I have overcome the world" (John 16:33 NKJV).

As believers, we know that God loves us and that He will protect us. In times of hardship, He will comfort us; in times of sorrow, He will dry our tears. When we are troubled, or weak, or sorrowful, God is always with us. We must build our lives on the rock that cannot be shaken: we must trust in God. And then, we must get on with the character-building, life-altering work of tackling our problems . . . because if we don't, who will? Or should?

A HEALTHY-CHOICE TIP

If you're trying to remodel yourself, you'll need to remodel your environment, too. In order to decrease temptations and increase the probability of success, you should take a long, hard look at your home, your office, and the places you frequently visit. Then, you must do whatever you can to move yourself as far as possible from the temptations that you intend to defeat.

DAY 25

ASKING FOR GOD'S HELP

So I say to you, ask, and it will be given to you; seek, and you will find; knock, and it will be opened to you. For everyone who asks receives, and he who seeks finds, and to him who knocks it will be opened.

Luke 11:9-10 NKJV

Do you genuinely want to strengthen your fitness and your faith? If the answer to that question is yes, then you should set aside ample time each morning to ask for God's help.

Today, make certain that you ask God specifically for the things you need.

Is prayer an integral part of your daily life, or is it a hit-or-miss habit? Do you "pray without ceasing," or is your prayer life an afterthought? Do you regularly pray in the quiet moments of the early morning, or do you bow your head only when others are watching?

As Christians, we are instructed to pray often. But it is important to note that genuine prayer requires much more than bending our knees and closing our eyes. Heartfelt prayer is an attitude of the heart.

If your prayers have become more a matter of habit than a matter of passion, you're robbing yourself of a deeper relationship with God. And how can you rectify that situation? By praying more frequently and more fervently.

When you do, God will shower you with His blessings, His grace, and His love.

FOOD FOR THOUGHT

A life growing in its purity and devotion will be a more prayerful life.

E. M. Bounds

God knows that we, with our limited vision, don't even know that for which we should pray. When we entrust our requests to him, we trust him to honor our prayers with holy judgment.

Max Lucado

When we are in the presence of God, removed from distractions, we are able to hear him more clearly, and a secure environment has been established for the young and broken places in our hearts to surface.

John Eldredge

STRENGTHENING YOUR FAITH

There's no corner of your life that's too unimportant to pray about, so pray about everything.

DAY 26

THE WORLD CHANGES, BUT GOD DOES NOT

There is a time for everything, and a season for every activity under heaven.

Ecclesiastes 3:1 NIV

Our world is in a state of constant change. God is not. At times, the world seems to be trembling beneath our feet. But we can be comforted in the knowledge that our Heavenly Father is the rock that cannot be shaken. His Word promises, "I am the Lord, I do not change" (Malachi 3:6 NKJV).

Every day that we live, we mortals encounter a multitude of changes—some good, some not so good. And on occasion, all of us must endure life-changing personal losses that leave us breathless. When we do, our loving Heavenly Father stands ready to protect us, to comfort us, to guide us, and, in time, to heal us.

Change is inevitable; growth is not. God will come to your doorstep on countless occasions with opportunities to learn and to grow.

Are you facing difficult circumstances or unwelcome changes? If so, please remember that God is far bigger than any problem you may face. So, instead of worrying about life's inevitable challenges, put your faith in the Father and His only begotten Son: "Jesus Christ is the same yesterday, today, and forever" (Hebrews 13:8 HCSB). And rest assured: It is precisely because your Savior does not change that you can face your challenges with courage for this day and hope for the future.

FOOD FOR THOUGHT

Mere change is not growth. Growth is the synthesis of change and continuity, and where there is no continuity there is no growth.

C. S. Lewis

In a world kept chaotic by change, you will eventually discover, as I have, that this is one of the most precious qualities of the God we are looking for: He doesn't change.

Bill Hybels

STRENGTHENING YOUR FAITH

Your journey with God unfolds day by day, and that's precisely how your journey to an improved state of physical fitness must also unfold: moment by moment, day by day, year by year.

DAY 27

REAL TRANSFORMATION? INNER TRANSFORMATION!

Therefore if anyone is in Christ, he is a new creature; the old things passed away; behold, new things have come.

2 Corinthians 5:17 HCSB

Have you invited God's Son to reign over your heart and your life? If so, think for a moment about the "old" you, the person you were before you invited Christ into your heart. Now, think about the "new" you, the person you have become since then. Is there a difference between the "old" you and the "new and improved" version? There should be! And that difference should be noticeable not only to you but also to others.

A true conversion experience results in a life transformed by Christ and a commitment to following in His footsteps.

Warren Wiersbe observed, "The greatest miracle of all is the transformation of a lost sinner into a child of God." And Oswald Chambers noted, "If the Spirit of God has transformed you within, you will exhibit Divine characteristics in your life, not good human characteristics. God's life in us expresses itself as God's life, not as a human life trying to be godly."

When you invited Christ to reign over your heart, you became a new creation through Him. This day offers yet another opportunity to behave yourself like that new creation by serving your Creator and strengthening your character. When you do, God will guide your steps and bless your endeavors today and forever.

FOOD FOR THOUGHT

No man is ever the same after God has laid His hand upon him.

A. W. Tozer

God wants to change our lives—and He will, as we open our hearts to Him.

Billy Graham

What is God looking for? He is looking for men and women whose hearts are completely His.

Charles Swindoll

A HEALTHY-CHOICE TIP

If you're serious about improving your fitness or your faith, pray about it.

DAY 28

GOD'S PROTECTION

The Lord is my strength and my song; He has become my salvation.

Exodus 15:2 HCSB

In a world filled with dangers and temptations, God is the ultimate armor. In a world filled with misleading messages, God's Word is the ultimate truth. In a world filled with more frustrations than we can count, God's Son offers the ultimate peace. Will you accept God's peace and wear God's armor against the dangers of our world?

Sometimes, in the crush of everyday life, God may seem far away, but He is not. God is everywhere you have ever been and everywhere you will ever go. He is with you night and day; He knows your thoughts and your prayers. He is your ultimate Protector. And, when you earnestly seek His protection, you will find it because He is here—always—waiting patiently for you to reach out to Him.

Today, pray for God's protection and God's guidance. You need both.

FOOD FOR THOUGHT

A God wise enough to create me and the world I live in is wise enough to watch out for me.

Philip Yancey

The Rock of Ages is the great sheltering encirclement.

Oswald Chambers

We are never out of reach of Satan's devices, so we must never be without the whole armor of God.

Warren Wiersbe

As sure as God puts his children in the furnace, he will be in the furnace with them.

C. H. *Spurgeon*

STRENGTHENING YOUR FAITH

You are protected by God . . . now and always. The only security that lasts is the security that flows from the loving heart of God.

DAY 29

BIG DREAMS

Looking at them, Jesus said, "With men it is impossible, but not with God, because all things are possible with God."

Mark 10:27 HCSB

Are you willing to entertain the possibility that God has big plans in store for you? Hopefully so. Yet sometimes, especially if you've recently experienced a life-altering disappointment, you may find it difficult to envision a brighter future for yourself and your family. If so, it's time to reconsider your own capabilities . . . and God's.

Your Heavenly Father created you with unique gifts and untapped talents; your job is to tap them. When you do, you'll begin to feel an increasing sense of confidence in yourself and in your future.

Be a dreamer: Your attitude toward the future will help create your future. So think realistically about yourself (and your situation) but focus your thoughts on hopes, not fears.

It takes courage to dream big dreams. You will discover that courage when you do three things: accept the past, trust God to handle the future, and make the most of the time He has given you today.

Nothing is too difficult for God, and no dreams are too big for Him—not even yours. So start living—and dreaming—accordingly.

FOOD FOR THOUGHT

You cannot out-dream God.

John Eldredge

To make your dream come true, you have to stay awake.

Dennis Swanberg

If you want to reach your potential, you need to add a strong work ethic to your talent.

John Maxwell

You were born with tremendous potential. When you were born again through faith in Jesus Christ, God added spiritual gifts to your natural talents.

Warren Wiersbe

A HEALTHY-CHOICE TIP

Educate yourself on which foods are healthy and which foods aren't. Read labels and learn the basics of proper nutrition. Then, use common sense and discipline in planning your diet.

DAY 30

PRAY CONSTANTLY ABOUT EVERYTHING, INCLUDING YOUR HEALTH

Rejoice always! Pray constantly. Give thanks in everything, for this is God's will for you in Christ Jesus.

1 Thessalonians 5:16-18 HCSB

Too many of us, even well-intentioned believers, tend to "compartmentalize" our waking hours into a few familiar categories: work, rest, play, family time, and worship. To do so is a mistake. Worship and praise should be woven into the fabric of our lives; prayer should never be relegated to a weekly three-hour visit to church on Sunday morning.

Theologian Wayne Oates once admitted, "Many of my prayers are made with my eyes open. You see, it seems I'm always praying about something, and it's not always convenient—or safe—to close my eyes." Dr. Oates understood that God always hears our prayers and that the relative position of our eyelids is of no concern to Him.

Today, spend time thinking about the power of prayer and the role that prayer plays in your life.

Today, find a little more time to lift your concerns to God in prayer, and praise. Pray about everything you can think of, including your spiritual, emotional, and physical health.

FOOD FOR THOUGHT

I am able to do all things through Him who strengthens me.

Philippians 4:13 HCSB

Prayer is never the least we can do; it is always the most!

A.W. *Tozer*

Pour out your heart to God and tell Him how you feel. Be real, be honest, and when you get it all out, you'll start to feel the gradual covering of God's comforting presence.

Bill Hybels

And He said to me, "My grace is sufficient for you, for My strength is made perfect in weakness."

2 Corinthians 12:9 NKJV

STRENGTHENING YOUR FAITH

When you've got a choice to make, pray about it—one way to make sure that your heart is in tune with God is to pray often. The more you talk to God, the more He will talk to you.

DAY 31

YOUR BODY, YOUR CHOICES

So then each of us shall give account of himself to God.

Romans 14:12 NKJV

As adults, each of us bears a personal responsibility for the general state of our own physical health. Certainly, various aspects of health are beyond our control: illness sometimes strikes even the healthiest men and women. But for most of us, physical health is a choice: it is the result of hundreds of small decisions that we make every day of our lives. If we make decisions that promote good health, our bodies respond. But if we fall into bad habits and undisciplined lifestyles, we suffer tragic consequences.

God has entrusted you with the responsibility of caring for your body . . . be proactive about your health.

When our unhealthy habits lead to poor health, we find it all too easy to look beyond ourselves and assign blame. In fact, we live in a society where blame has become a national obsession: we blame cigarette manufacturers, restaurants, and food producers, to name only a few. But to blame others is to miss the point: we, and we alone, are responsible for the way that we treat our bodies. And the sooner that we accept that responsibility, the sooner we can assert control over our bodies and our lives.

Do you sincerely desire to improve your physical fitness? If so, start by taking personal responsibility for the body that God has given you. Then, make the solemn pledge to yourself that you will begin to make the changes that are required to enjoy a longer, healthier, happier life.

FOOD FOR THOUGHT

Even a child is known by his actions, by whether his conduct is pure and right.

Proverbs 20:11 NIV

Do not pray for easy lives. Pray to be stronger men! Do not pray for tasks equal to your powers. Pray for powers equal to your tasks.

Phillips Brooks

A HEALTHY-CHOICE TIP

It's easy to blame other people for the current state of your health. You live in a world where it's fashionable to blame food manufacturers, doctors, and fast food restaurants, to mention but a few. Yet none of these folks force food into your mouth, and they don't force you to sit on the sofa when you should be exercising! So remember: it's your body . . . and it's your responsibility.

DAY 32

MAKING THE RIGHT CHOICES

A wise man will hear and increase learning, and a man of understanding will attain wise counsel.

Proverbs 1:5 NKJV

Life is a series of choices. Each day, we make countless decisions that can bring us closer to God . . . or not. When we live according to God's commandments, we earn for ourselves the abundance and peace that He intends for us to experience. But, when we turn our backs upon God by disobeying Him, we bring needless suffering upon ourselves and our families.

Today, think about unwise choices you've made in the past and wise choices you intend to make in the future.

Do you seek God's peace and His blessings? Then obey Him. When you're faced with a difficult choice or a powerful temptation, seek God's counsel and trust the counsel He gives. Invite God into your heart and live according to His commandments. When you do, you will be blessed today, tomorrow, and forever.

God has given you a guidebook for righteous living called the Holy Bible. It contains thorough instructions which, if followed, lead to fulfillment and salvation. But, if you choose to ignore God's commandments, the results are as predictable as they are tragic.

So here's a surefire formula for a happy, abundant life: live righteously. For further instructions, read the manual.

FOOD FOR THOUGHT

Wisdom is the God-given ability to see life with rare objectivity and to handle life with rare stability.

Charles Swindoll

The essence of wisdom, from a practical standpoint, is pausing long enough to look at our lives—invitations, opportunities, relationships—from God's perspective. And then acting on it.

Charles Stanley

A HEALTHY-CHOICE TIP

John Maxwell observed, "The key to healthy eating is moderation and managing what you eat every day." And he was right. Crash diets don't usually work, but sensible eating habits do work, so plan your meals accordingly.

DAY 33

HEALTHY PRIORITIES

Beloved, I pray that in all respects you may prosper and be in good health, just as your soul prospers.

3 John 1:2 NASB

When it comes to matters of physical, spiritual, and emotional health, Christians possess an infallible guidebook: the Holy Bible. And, when it comes to matters concerning fitness—whether physical, emotional, or spiritual fitness—God's Word can help us establish clear priorities that can guide our steps and our lives.

Time is a non-renewable resource. Today, think about the ways to spend your time more wisely.

It's easy to talk about establishing clear priorities for maintaining physical and spiritual health, but it's much more difficult to live according to those priorities. For busy believers living in a demanding world, placing first things first can be difficult indeed. Why? Because so many people are expecting so many things from us!

If you're having trouble prioritizing your day—or if you're having trouble sticking to a plan that enhances your spiritual and physical health—perhaps you've been trying to organize your life according to your own plans, not God's. A better strategy, of course, is to take your daily obligations and place them in the hands of the One who created you. To do so, you must prioritize your day according to God's commandments, and you must seek His will and His wisdom in all matters.

FOOD FOR THOUGHT

Ultimate healing and the glorification of the body are certainly among the blessings of Calvary for the believing Christian. Immediate healing is not guaranteed.

Warren Wiersbe

A HEALTHY-CHOICE TIP

High blood pressure can cause heart attacks, strokes, and plenty of other serious health problems. The good news is that high blood pressure is usually treatable with medication, or lifestyle changes, or both. But you won't know you need treatment unless you know your blood pressure. Thankfully, blood pressure cuffs can be found just about everywhere, in many drug stores and even in some supermarkets. So remember this: you don't have to wait for a doctor's appointment to check your blood pressure. You can monitor your own blood pressure in between visits to the doctor's office, and that's precisely what you should do.

DAY 34

GETTING ENOUGH REST?

Come to Me, all you who are weary and burdened, and I will give you rest.

Matthew 11:28-30 NKJV

Even the most inspired Christians can, from time to time, find themselves running on empty. The demands of daily life can drain us of our strength and rob us of the joy that is rightfully ours in Christ. When we find ourselves tired, discouraged, or worse, there is a source from which we can draw the power needed to recharge our spiritual batteries. That source is God.

God wants you to get enough rest. The world wants you to burn the candle at both ends. Trust God.

God intends that His children lead joyous lives filled with abundance and peace. But sometimes, abundance and peace seem very far away. It is then that we must turn to God for renewal, and when we do, He will restore us.

God expects us to work hard, but He also intends for us to rest. When we fail to take the rest that we need, we do a disservice to ourselves and to our families.

Is your spiritual battery running low? Is your energy on the wane? Are your emotions frayed? If so, it's time to turn your thoughts and your prayers to God.

FOOD FOR THOUGHT

I said to myself, "Relax and rest. God has showered you with blessings."

Psalm 116:7 MSG

And be not conformed to this world: but be ye transformed by the renewing of your mind.

Romans 12:2 KJV

And the apostles gathered themselves together unto Jesus, and told him all things, both what they had done, and what they had taught. And he said unto them, Come ye yourselves apart into a desert place, and rest a while.

Mark 6:30-31 HCSB

I will lift up mine eyes unto the hills, from whence cometh my help. My help cometh from the Lord, which made heaven and earth.

Psalm 121:1-2 KJV

A HEALTHY-CHOICE TIP

Most adults need about eight hours of sleep each night. If you're depriving yourself of much needed sleep in order to stay up and watch late night television, you've developed a bad habit. Instead, do yourself a favor: turn off the TV and go to bed.

DAY 35

MISDIRECTED WORSHIP: THE TRAGEDY OF ADDICTION

Let us walk with decency, as in the daylight: not in carousing and drunkenness.

Romans 13:13 HCSB

The dictionary defines addiction as "the compulsive need for a habit-forming substance; the condition of being habitually and compulsively occupied with something." That definition is accurate, but incomplete. For Christians, addiction has an additional meaning: it means compulsively worshipping something other than God.

You must guard your heart against addiction . . . or else.

Ours is a highly addictive society. Why? The answer is straightforward: supply and demand. The supply of addictive substances continues to grow; the affordability and availability of these substances makes them highly attractive to consumers; and the overall demand for addictive substances has increased as more and more users have become addicted to an ever-expanding array of substances and compulsions.

You know people who are full-blown addicts—probably lots of people. If you, or someone you love, is suffering from the blight of addiction, the following ideas are worth remembering:

1. For the addict, addiction comes first. In the life of an addict, addiction rules. God, of course, commands otherwise. God says, "You shall have no other gods before Me," and He means precisely what He says (Exodus 20:3 NKJV). Our task, as believers, is to put God in His proper place: first place. 2. You cannot cure another person's addiction, but you can encourage that person to seek help. Addicts are cured when they decide, not when you decide. What you can do is this: you can be supportive, and you can encourage the addict to find the help that he or she needs (Luke 10:25-37). 3. If you are living with an addicted person, think about safety: yours and your family's. Addiction is life-threatening and life-shortening. Don't let someone else's addiction threaten your safety or the safety of your loved ones (Proverbs 22:3). 4. Don't assist in prolonging the addiction: When you interfere with the negative consequences that might otherwise accompany an addict's negative behaviors, you are inadvertently "enabling" the addict to continue the destructive cycle of addiction. So don't be an enabler (Proverbs 15:31). 5. Help is available: Lots of people have experienced addiction and lived to tell about it. They want to help. Let them (Proverbs 27:17). 6. A cure is possible. With God's help, no addiction is incurable. And with God, no situation is hopeless (Matthew 19:26).

DAY 36

THE POWER OF DAILY WORSHIP AND MEDITATION

Man shall not live by bread alone, but by every word that proceeds from the mouth of God.

Matthew 4:4 NKJV

Are you concerned about your spiritual, physical, or emotional fitness? If so, there is a timeless source of advice and comfort upon which you can—and should—depend. That source is the Holy Bible.

God's Word has much to say about every aspect of your life, including your health. If you face personal health challenges that seem almost insoluble, have faith and seek God's wisdom. If you can't seem to get yourself on a sensible diet or on a program of regular physical exercise, consult God's teachings. If your approach to your physical or emotional health has, up to this point, been undisciplined, pray for the strength to do what you know is right.

God's Word has the power to change every aspect of your life, including your health.

God has given you the Holy Bible for the purpose of knowing His promises, His power, His commandments, His wisdom, His love, and His Son. As you seek to improve the state of your own health, study God's teachings and apply them to your life. When you do, you will be blessed, now and forever.

FOOD FOR THOUGHT

He awakens Me morning by morning, He awakens My ear to hear as the learned. The Lord God has opened My ear.

Isaiah 50:4-5 NKJV

Lord, You are my lamp; the Lord illuminates my darkness.

2 Samuel 22:29 HCSB

Teach me Your way, Lord, and I will live by Your truth. Give me an undivided mind to fear Your name.

Psalm 86:11 HCSB

I will instruct you and show you the way to go; with My eye on you, I will give counsel.

Psalm 32:8 HCSB

STRENGTHENING YOUR FAITH

Find the best time of the day to spend with God. Hudson Taylor, an English missionary, wrote, "Whatever is your best time in the day, give that to communion with God." That's powerful advice that leads to a powerful faith.

DAY 37

THE FUTILITY OF BLAME

People's own foolishness ruins their lives, but in their minds they blame the Lord.

Proverbs 19:3 NCV

When our unhealthy habits lead to poor health, we find it all too easy to look beyond ourselves and assign blame. In fact, we live in a society where blame has become a national obsession: we blame cigarette manufacturers, restaurants, and food producers, to name only a few. But to blame others is to miss the point: we, and we alone, are responsible for the way that we treat our bodies. And the sooner that we accept that responsibility, the sooner we can assert control over our bodies and our lives.

So, when it comes to your own body, assume control and accept responsibility. It's a great way to live and a great way to stay healthy.

Today, ask God to help you take responsibility for the current state of your health. And while you're at it, ask Him to help you make wise choices in the future.

FOOD FOR THOUGHT

The main thing is this: we should never blame anyone or anything for our defeats. No matter how evil their intentions may be, they are altogether unable to harm us until we begin to blame them and use them as excuses for our own unbelief.

A. W. Tozer

The single most important element in any human relationship is honesty—with oneself, with God, and with others.

Catherine Marshall

Never use your problem as an excuse for bad attitudes or behavior.

Joyce Meyer

A HEALTHY-CHOICE TIP

Do you think God wants you to develop healthy habits? Of course He does! Physical, emotional, and spiritual fitness are all part of God's plan for you. But it's up to you to make certain that a healthy lifestyle is a fundamental part of your plan, too.

DAY 38

YOUR CHOICES MATTER

I am offering you life or death, blessings or curses. Now, choose life! . . . To choose life is to love the Lord your God, obey him, and stay close to him.

Deuteronomy 30:19-20 NCV

Each day, we make thousands of small choices concerning the things that we do and the things we think. Most of these choices are made without too much forethought. In fact, most of us go about our daily lives spending a significant portion of our lives simply reacting to events. Often, our actions are simply the result of impulse or habit. God asks that we slow down long enough to think about the choices that we make, and He asks that we make those choices in accordance with His commandments.

First you make choices . . . and soon those choices begin to shape your life. That's why you must make smart choices . . . or face the consequences.

The Bible teaches us that our bodies are "temples" that belong to God (1 Corinthians 6:19-20). We are commanded (not encouraged, not advised, commanded!) to treat our bodies with respect and honor. We do so by making wise choices and by making those choices consistently over an extended period of time.

Do you sincerely seek to improve the overall quality of your health? Then vow to yourself and to God that you will begin making the kind of wise choices that will lead to a longer, healthier, happier life. The responsibility for those choices is yours. And so are the rewards.

FOOD FOR THOUGHT

Every time you make a choice, you are turning the central part of you, the part that chooses, into something a little different from what it was before.

C. S. Lewis

Life is pretty much like a cafeteria line—it offers us many choices, both good and bad. The Christian must have a spiritual radar that detects the difference not only between bad and good but also among good, better, and best.

Dennis Swanberg

A HEALTHY-CHOICE TIP

The road to poor health is paved with good intentions. Until you make exercise a high priority in your life, your good intentions will soon give way to old habits. So give your exercise regimen a position of high standing on your daily to-do list.

DAY 39

FINDING CONTENTMENT

I have learned to be content in whatever circumstances I am.

Philippians 4:11 HCSB

> Contentment is possible when we stop striving for more.
>
> *Charles Swindoll*

When we conduct ourselves in ways that are opposed to God's commandments, we rob ourselves of God's peace. When we fall prey to the temptations and distractions of our irreverent age, we rob ourselves of God's blessings. When we become preoccupied with material possessions or personal status, we forfeit the contentment that is rightfully ours in Christ.

Where can we find the kind of contentment that Paul describes in Philippians 4:12-13? Is it a result of wealth, power, or fame? Hardly. Genuine contentment is a gift from God to those who follow His commandments and accept His Son. When Christ dwells at the center of our families and our lives, contentment will belong to us just as surely as we belong to Him.

Are you a contented Christian? If so, then you're well aware of the healing power of the risen Christ. But if your spirit is temporarily troubled, perhaps you need to focus less upon your own priorities and more upon God's priorities. When you do, you'll rediscover this life-changing truth: Genuine contentment begins with God . . . and ends there.

FOOD FOR THOUGHT

Real contentment hinges on what's happening inside us, not around us.

Charles Stanley

Nobody who gets enough food and clothing in a world where most are hungry and cold has any business to talk about "misery."

C. S. *Lewis*

What a shame it will be if those who have the grace of God within them should fall short of the contentment which worldly men have attained.

C. H. *Spurgeon*

STRENGTHENING YOUR FAITH

Be contented where you are, even if it's not exactly where you want to end up. God has something wonderful in store for you—and remember that God's timing is perfect—so be patient, trust God, do your best, and expect the best.

DAY 40

KNOW WHAT YOU EAT

Acquire wisdom—how much better it is than gold! And acquire understanding—it is preferable to silver.

Proverbs 16:16 HCSB

How hard is it for us to know the nutritional properties of the foods we eat? Not very hard. In the grocery store, almost every food item is clearly marked. In fast-food restaurants, the fat and calorie contents are posted on the wall (although the print is incredibly small, and with good reason: the health properties of these tasty tidbits are, in most cases, so poor that we should rename them "fat foods").

As informed adults, we have access to all the information that we need to make healthy dietary choices. Now it's up to each of us to make wise dietary choices, or not. Those choices are ours, and so are their consequences.

Today, make it a point to measure every calorie you consume. Then, at the end of the day, ask yourself if your food choices have been wise.

FOOD FOR THOUGHT

But also for this very reason, giving all diligence, add to your faith virtue, to virtue knowledge.

2 Peter 1:5 NKJV

Let the word of Christ dwell in you richly in all wisdom, teaching and admonishing one another in psalms and hymns and spiritual songs, singing with grace in your hearts to the Lord.

Colossians 3:16 NKJV

Those who are wise shall shine like the brightness of the firmament, and those who turn many to righteousness like the stars forever and ever.

Daniel 12:3 NKJV

STRENGTHENING YOUR FAITH

Wisdom 101: If you're looking for wisdom (health or otherwise), the Book of Proverbs is a wonderful place to start. It has 31 chapters, one for each day of the month. If you read Proverbs regularly, and if you take its teachings to heart, you'll gain timeless wisdom from God's unchanging Word.

DAY 41

BE ENTHUSIASTIC

Whatever you do, do it enthusiastically, as something done for the Lord and not for men.

Colossians 3:23 HCSB

Are you passionate about your faith, your fitness, and your future? Hopefully so. But if your zest for life has waned, it is now time to redirect your efforts and recharge your spiritual batteries. And that means refocusing your priorities by putting God first.

Each day is a glorious opportunity to serve God and to do His will. Are you enthused about life, or do you struggle through each day giving scarcely a thought to God's blessings? Are you constantly praising God for His gifts, and are you sharing His Good News with the world? And are you excited about the possibilities for service that God has placed before you, whether at home, at work, or at church? You should be.

Look at your life and your challenges as exciting adventures. Don't wait for life to spice itself; spice things up yourself.

Nothing is more important than your wholehearted commitment to your Creator and to His only begotten Son. Your faith must never be an afterthought; it must be your ultimate priority, your ultimate possession, and your ultimate passion. When you become passionate about your faith, you'll become passionate about your life, too.

FOOD FOR THOUGHT

Wherever you are, be all there. Live to the hilt every situation you believe to be the will of God.

Jim Elliot

Catch on fire with enthusiasm and people will come for miles to watch you burn.

John Wesley

A HEALTHY-CHOICE TIP

You don't have to attend medical school to understand the basic principles of maintaining a healthy lifestyle. In fact, many of the things you need to know are contained in this text. But don't stop here. Vow to make yourself an expert on the care and feeding of the body that God has given you. In today's information-packed world, becoming an expert isn't a very hard thing to do.

DAY 42

START MAKING CHANGES NOW!

But be doers of the word and not hearers only.

James 1:22 HCSB

Warren Wiersbe correctly observed, "A Christian should no more defile his body than a Jew would defile the temple." Unfortunately, too many of us have allowed our temples to fall into disrepair. When it comes to fitness and food, it's easy to fall into bad habits. And it's easy to convince ourselves that we'll start improving our health "some day."

Today, pick out one important obligation that you've been putting off. Then, take at least one specific step toward the completion of it.

If we are to care for our bodies in the way that God intends, we must establish healthy habits, and we must establish them sooner rather than later.

Saint Jerome advised, "Begin to be now what you will be hereafter." You should take his advice seriously, and you should take it NOW. When it comes to your health, it's always the right time to start establishing the right habits.

FOOD FOR THOUGHT

Let us not be content to wait and see what will happen, but give us the determination to make the right things happen.

Peter Marshall

Therefore, get your minds ready for action, being self-disciplined, and set your hope completely on the grace to be brought to you at the revelation of Jesus Christ.

1 Peter 1:13 HCSB

When you make a vow to God, don't delay fulfilling it, because He does not delight in fools. Fulfill what you vow.

Ecclesiastes 5:4 HCSB

For the hearers of the law are not righteous before God, but the doers of the law will be declared righteous.

Romans 2:13 HCSB

A HEALTHY-CHOICE TIP

When important work needs to be done, it's tempting to procrastinate. But God's Word teaches us to be "doers of the Word," which means taking action even when we might prefer to do nothing.

DAY 43

PROTECTING YOUR EMOTIONAL HEALTH

And the peace of God, which surpasses every thought, will guard your hearts and your minds in Christ Jesus. Finally brothers, whatever is true, whatever is honorable, whatever is just, whatever is pure, whatever is lovely, whatever is commendable—if there is any moral excellence and if there is any praise—dwell on these things.

Philippians 4:7-8 HCSB

Emotional health isn't simply the absence of sadness; it's also the ability to enjoy life and the wisdom to celebrate God's gifts. Christians have every reason to be optimistic about life. As John Calvin observed, "There is not one blade of grass, there is no color in this world that is not intended to make us rejoice." But sometimes, when we are tired or frustrated, rejoicing seems only a distant promise. Thankfully, God stands ready to restore us: "I will give you a new heart and put a new spirit in you...." (Ezekiel 36:26 NIV). Our task, of course, is to let Him.

When negative emotions threaten to hijack your day, lift your thoughts and your prayers to God.

If you're feeling deeply discouraged or profoundly depressed, then it is time to seriously address the state of your emotional health. First, open your heart to

God in prayer. Then, talk with trusted family members, friends, and your pastor. And, if you or someone close to you considers it wise, seek advice from your physician or make an appointment with a licensed mental health professional.

When your emotional health is at stake, you should avail yourself of every reasonable resource. Then, armed with the promises of your Creator and the support of family and friends, you can go about the business of solving the challenges that confront you. When you do, the clouds will eventually part, and the sun will shine once more upon your soul.

FOOD FOR THOUGHT

The busier we are, the easier it is to worry, the greater the temptation to worry, the greater the need to be alone with God.

Charles Stanley

A HEALTHY-CHOICE TIP

John Maxwell observed, "The key to healthy eating is moderation and managing what you eat every day." And he was right. Crash diets don't usually work, but sensible eating habits do work, so plan your meals accordingly.

DAY 44

SENSIBLE EXERCISE

No discipline seems pleasant at the time, but painful. Later on, however, it produces a harvest of righteousness and peace for those who have been trained by it.

Hebrews 12:11 NIV

A healthy lifestyle includes regular, sensible physical exercise. How much exercise is right for you? That's a decision that you should make in consultation with your physician. But make no mistake: if you sincerely desire to be a thoughtful caretaker of the body that God has given you, exercise is important.

God rewards wise behaviors and He punishes misbehavior. A commitment to a sensible exercise program is one way of being wise, and it's also one way of pleasing God.

Once you begin a regular exercise program, you'll discover that the benefits to you are not only physical but also psychological. Regular exercise allows you to build your muscles while you're clearing your head and lifting your spirits.

So, if you've been taking your body for granted, today is a wonderful day to change. You can start slowly, perhaps with a brisk walk around the block. As your stamina begins to build, so will your sense of satisfaction. And, you'll be comforted by the knowledge that you've done your part to protect and preserve the precious body that God has entrusted to your care.

FOOD FOR THOUGHT

The effective Christians of history have been men and women of great personal discipline—mental discipline, discipline of the body, discipline of the tongue, and discipline of the emotion.

Billy Graham

Sow righteousness for yourselves and reap faithful love; break up your untilled ground. It is time to seek the Lord until He comes and sends righteousness on you like the rain.

Hosea 10:12 HCSB

Don't you know that you are God's temple and that God's Spirit lives in you?

1 Corinthians 3:16 NCV

A HEALTHY-CHOICE TIP

Make exercise enjoyable. Your workouts should be a source of pleasure and satisfaction, not a form of self-imposed punishment. Find a way to exercise your body that is satisfying, effective, and fun.

DAY 45

SPIRITUAL HEALTH, SPIRITUAL GROWTH

But the fruit of the Spirit is love, joy, peace, long-suffering, gentleness, goodness, faith, meekness, temperance . . . .

Galatians 5:22-23 KJV

Are you as "spiritually fit" as you're ever going to be? Hopefully not! When it comes to your faith (and, by the way, when it comes to your fitness), God isn't done with you yet.

Wherever you are in your spiritual journey, it's always the right time to take another step toward God.

The journey toward spiritual maturity lasts a lifetime: As Christians, we can and should continue to grow in the love and the knowledge of our Savior as long as we live. But, if we cease to grow, either emotionally or spiritually, we do ourselves and our families a profound disservice.

If we study God's Word, if we obey His commandments, and if we live in the center of His will, we will not be "stagnant" believers; we will, instead, be growing Christians . . . and that's exactly what God wants for our lives.

In those quiet moments when we open our hearts to God, the Creator who made us keeps remaking us. He gives us direction, perspective, wisdom, and courage. He encourages us to become more fit in a variety of ways:

more spiritually fit, more physically fit, and more emotionally fit.

God is willing to do His part to ensure that you remain fit. Are you willing to do yours?

FOOD FOR THOUGHT

A Christian is never in a state of completion but always in the process of becoming.

Martin Luther

When you and I hurt deeply, what we really need is not an explanation from God but a revelation of God. We need to see how great God is; we need to recover our lost perspective on life. Things get out of proportion when we are suffering, and it takes a vision of something bigger than ourselves to get life's dimensions adjusted again.

Warren Wiersbe

STRENGTHENING YOUR FAITH

Spiritual growth is not instantaneous . . . and neither, for that matter, is the attainment of a physically fit body. So be patient. You should expect a few ups and downs along the way, but you should also expect to see progress over time.

DAY 46

HAVE THE COURAGE TO TRUST GOD

Trust in the Lord with all your heart, and do not rely on your own understanding; think about Him in all your ways, and He will guide you on the right paths.

Proverbs 3:5-6 HCSB

When our dreams come true and our plans prove successful, we find it easy to thank our Creator and easy to trust His divine providence. But in times of sorrow or hardship, we may find ourselves questioning God's plans for our lives.

On occasion, you will confront circumstances that trouble you to the very core of your soul. It is during these difficult days that you must find the wisdom and the courage to trust your Heavenly Father despite your circumstances.

Are you a man who seeks God's blessings for yourself and your family? Then trust Him. Trust Him with your relationships. Trust Him with your priorities. Follow His commandments and pray for His guidance. Trust Your Heavenly Father day by day, moment by moment—in good times and in trying times. Then, wait patiently for God's revelations . . .

Sometimes the very essence of faith is trusting God in the midst of things He knows good and well we cannot comprehend.

Beth Moore

and prepare yourself for the abundance and peace that will most certainly be yours when you do.

FOOD FOR THOUGHT

Are you serious about wanting God's guidance to become the person he wants you to be? The first step is to tell God that you know you can't manage your own life; that you need his help.

Catherine Marshall

Do not be afraid, then, that if you trust, or tell others to trust, the matter will end there. Trust is only the beginning and the continual foundation. When we trust Him, the Lord works, and His work is the important part of the whole matter.

Hannah Whitall Smith

STRENGTHENING YOUR FAITH

Because God is trustworthy—and because He has made promises to you that He intends to keep—you are protected.

DAY 47

IN SEARCH OF WISDOM AND BALANCE

Now if any of you lacks wisdom, he should ask God, who gives to all generously and without criticizing, and it will be given to him. But let him ask in faith without doubting. For the doubter is like the surging sea, driven and tossed by the wind.

James 1:5-6 HCSB

To find balance, you must find wisdom. Where will you find wisdom today? Will you seek it from God or from the world? As a thoughtful man living in a society that is filled with temptations and distractions, you know that the world's brand of "wisdom" is everywhere . . . and it is dangerous. You live in a world where it's all too easy to stray far from the ultimate source of wisdom: God's Holy Word.

God makes His wisdom available to you. Your job is to acknowledge, to understand, and (above all) to use that wisdom.

When you commit yourself to the daily study of God's Word—and when you live according to His commandments—you will become wise . . . in time. But don't expect to open your Bible today and be wise tomorrow. Wisdom is not like a mushroom; it does not spring up overnight. It is, instead, like a majestic oak tree that starts as a tiny acorn, grows into a sapling, and eventually reaches up to the sky, tall and strong.

Today and every day, as a way of understanding God's plan for your life, you should study His Word and live by it. When you do, you will accumulate a storehouse of wisdom that will enrich your own life and the lives of your family members, your friends, and the world.

FOOD FOR THOUGHT

Wisdom is knowledge applied. Head knowledge is useless on the battlefield. Knowledge stamped on the heart makes one wise.

Beth Moore

If we neglect the Bible, we cannot expect to benefit from the wisdom and direction that result from knowing God's Word.

Vonette Bright

A HEALTHY-CHOICE TIP

An exercise program that starts slowly and builds over time is far better than an exercise program that starts—and ends—quickly.

DAY 48

PRAY CONSTANTLY

Rejoice in hope; be patient in affliction; be persistent in prayer.

Romans 12:12 HCSB

God's Word promises that prayer is a powerful tool for changing your life and your world. So here's a question: Are you using prayer as a powerful tool to improve your world, or are you praying sporadically at best? If you're wise, you've learned that prayer is indeed powerful and that it is most powerful when it is used often.

If you need something, don't ask for God's help in general terms; ask specifically for the things you need.

Today, if you haven't already done so, establish the habit of praying constantly. Don't pray day-to-day; pray hour-to-hour. Start each day with prayer, end it with prayer, and fill it with prayer. That's the best way to know God; it's the best way to change your world; and it is, quite simply, the best way to live.

FOOD FOR THOUGHT

God shapes the world by prayer. The more praying there is in the world, the better the world will be, and the mightier will be the forces against evil.

E. M. Bounds

Prayer shouldn't be casual or sporadic, dictated only by the needs of the moment. Prayer should be as much a part of our lives as breathing.

Billy Graham

We must leave it to God to answer our prayers in His own wisest way. Sometimes, we are so impatient and think that God does not answer. God always answers! He never fails! Be still. Abide in Him.

Mrs. Charles E. Cowman

STRENGTHENING YOUR FAITH

When you've got a choice to make, pray about it—one way to make sure that your heart is in tune with God is to pray often. The more you talk to God, the more He will talk to you.

DAY 49

FOLLOWING HIS FOOTSTEPS

"Follow Me," Jesus told them, "and I will make you into fishers of men!" Immediately they left their nets and followed Him.

Mark 1:17-18 HCSB

Jesus walks with you. Are you walking with Him? Hopefully, you will choose to walk with Him today and every day of your life.

Jesus loved you so much that He endured unspeakable humiliation and suffering for you. How will you respond to Christ's sacrifice? Will you take up His cross and follow Him (Luke 9:23), or will you choose another path? When you place your hopes squarely at the foot of the cross, when you place Jesus squarely at the center of your life, you will be blessed.

If you want to be a little more like Jesus . . . learn about His teachings, follow in His footsteps, and obey His commandments.

The old familiar hymn begins, "What a friend we have in Jesus...." No truer words were ever penned. Jesus is the sovereign Friend and ultimate Savior of mankind. Christ showed enduring love for His believers by willingly sacrificing His own life so that we might have eternal life. Now, it is our turn to become His friend.

Let us love our Savior, let us praise Him, and let us share His message of salvation with the world. When we do, we demonstrate that our acquaintance with the Master is not a passing fancy, but is, instead, the cornerstone and the touchstone of our lives.

FOOD FOR THOUGHT

Our responsibility is to feed from Him, to stay close to Him, to follow Him—because sheep easily go astray—so that we eternally experience the protection and companionship of our Great Shepherd the Lord Jesus Christ.

Franklin Graham

Look for yourself, and you will find in the long run only hatred, loneliness, despair, rage, ruin and decay. But look for Christ, and you will find Him, and with Him everything else thrown in.

C. S. Lewis

STRENGTHENING YOUR FAITH

Following Christ is a matter of obedience. If you want to be a little more like Jesus . . . learn about His teachings, follow in His footsteps, and obey His commandments.

DAY 50

TRUSTING GOD'S WILL

God is my shield, saving those whose hearts are true and right.

Psalm 7:10 NLT

God has will, and so do we. He gave us the power to make choices for ourselves, and He created a world in which those choices have consequences. The ultimate choice that we face, of course, is what to do about God. We can cast our lot with Him by choosing Jesus Christ as our personal Savior, or not. The choice is ours alone.

We also face thousands of small choices that make up the fabric of daily life. When we align those choices with God's commandments, and when we align our lives with God's will, we receive His abundance, His peace, and His joy. But when we struggle against God's will for our lives, we reap a bitter harvest indeed.

When God's will becomes your will, good things happen.

Today, you'll face thousands of small choices; as you do, use God's Word as your guide. And, as you face the ultimate choice, place God's Son and God's will and God's love at the center of your life. You'll discover that God's plan is far grander than any you could have imagined.

FOOD FOR THOUGHT

Our sense of joy, satisfaction, and fulfillment in life increases, no matter what the circumstances, if we are in the center of God's will.

Billy Graham

To walk out of His will is to walk into nowhere.

C. S. Lewis

Absolute submission is not enough; we should go on to joyful acquiescence to the will of God.

C. H. Spurgeon

In times of uncertainty, wait. Always, if you have any doubt, wait. Do not force yourself to any action. If you have a restraint in your spirit, wait until all is clear, and do not go against it.

Mrs. Charles E. Cowman

A HEALTHY-CHOICE TIP

Exercising discipline should never be viewed as an imposition or as a form of punishment; far from it. Discipline is the means by which you can take control of your life (which, by the way, is far better than letting your life control you).

DAY 51

NEED SOMETHING FROM GOD? ASK!

You do not have because you do not ask.

James 4:2 HCSB

How often do you ask God for His help and His wisdom? Occasionally? Intermittently? Whenever you experience a crisis? Hopefully not. Hopefully, you've acquired the habit of asking for God's assistance early and often. And hopefully, you have learned to seek His guidance in every aspect of your life.

Think of a specific need that is weighing heavily on your heart. Then, spend a few quiet moments asking God for His guidance and for His help.

Jesus made it clear to His disciples: they should petition God to meet their needs. So should you. Genuine, heartfelt prayer produces powerful changes in you and in your world. When you lift your heart to God, you open yourself to a never-ending source of divine wisdom and infinite love.

James 5:16 makes a promise that God intends to keep: when you pray earnestly, fervently, and often, great things will happen. Too many people, however, are too timid or too pessimistic to ask God to do big things. Please don't count yourself among their number.

God can do great things through you if you have the courage to ask Him (and the determination to keep asking Him). But don't expect Him to do all the work. When you do your part, He will do His part—and when He does, you can expect miracles to happen.

The Bible promises that God will guide you if you let Him. Your job is to let Him. But sometimes, you will be tempted to do otherwise. Sometimes, you'll be tempted to go along with the crowd; other times, you'll be tempted to do things your way, not God's way. When you feel those temptations, resist them.

God has promised that when you ask for His help, He will not withhold it. So ask. Ask Him to meet the needs of your day. Ask Him to lead you, to protect you, and to correct you. Then, trust the answers He gives.

God stands at the door and waits. When you knock, He opens. When you ask, He answers. Your task, of course, is to make God a full partner in every aspect of your life—and to seek His guidance prayerfully and often.

A HEALTHY-CHOICE TIP

If you want more from life, ask more from God. If you're searching for peace and abundance, ask for God's help—and keep asking—until He answers your prayers. If you sincerely want to rise above the stresses and complications of everyday life, ask for God's help many times each day.

DAY 52

KEEPING UP APPEARANCES

For am I now trying to win the favor of people, or God? Or am I striving to please people? If I were still trying to please people, I would not be a slave of Christ.

Galatians 1:10 HCSB

Are you worried about keeping up appearances? And as a result, do you spend too much time, energy, or money on things that are intended to make you look good? If so, you are certainly not alone. Ours is a society that focuses intently upon appearances. We are told time and again that we can't be "too thin or too rich." But in truth, the important things in life have little to do with food, fashion, fame, or fortune.

When making judgments about yourself and others, don't focus on appearances, focus on values.

Today, spend less time trying to please the world and more time trying to please your earthly family and your Father in heaven. Focus on pleasing your God and your loved ones, and don't worry too much about trying to impress the folks you happen to pass on the street. It takes too much energy—and too much life—to keep up appearances. So don't waste your energy or your life.

FOOD FOR THOUGHT

If the narrative of the Scriptures teaches us anything, from the serpent in the Garden to the carpenter in Nazareth, it teaches us that things are rarely what they seem, that we shouldn't be fooled by appearances.

John Eldredge

The single most important element in any human relationship is honesty—with oneself, with God, and with others.

Catherine Marshall

Don't be addicted to approval. Follow your heart. Do what you believe God is telling you to do, and stand firm in Him and Him alone.

Joyce Meyer

A HEALTHY-CHOICE TIP

Appearances, appearances, appearances: don't be too worried about what you look like on the outside—be more concerned about the kind of person you are on the inside. And while you're at it, don't judge other people by their appearances, either.

DAY 53

CELEBRATION!

Celebrate God all day, every day. I mean, revel in him!

Philippians 4:4 MSG

God gives us this day; He fills it to the brim with possibilities, and He challenges us to use it for His purposes. The 118th Psalm reminds us that today, like every other day, is a cause for celebration. The day is presented to us fresh and clean at midnight, free of charge, but we must beware: Today is a non-renewable resource—once it's gone, it's gone forever. Our responsibility, of course, is to use this day in the service of God's will and according to His commandments.

By celebrating the gift of life, you protect your heart from the dangers of pessimism, regret, hopelessness, and bitterness.

Today, treasure the time that God has given you. Give Him the glory and the praise and the thanksgiving that He deserves. And search for the hidden possibilities that God has placed along your path. This day is a priceless gift from God, so use it joyfully and encourage others to do likewise. After all, this is the day the Lord has made.

FOOD FOR THOUGHT

Joy is the direct result of having God's perspective on our daily lives and the effect of loving our Lord enough to obey His commands and trust His promises.

Bill Bright

Our sense of joy, satisfaction, and fulfillment in life increases, no matter what the circumstances, if we are in the center of God's will.

Billy Graham

A life of intimacy with God is characterized by joy.

Oswald Chambers

When we get rid of inner conflicts and wrong attitudes toward life, we will almost automatically burst into joy.

E. Stanley Jones

STRENGTHENING YOUR FAITH

God has given you the gift of life (here on earth) and the promise of eternal life (in heaven). Now, He wants you to celebrate those gifts. By celebrating the gift of life, you protect your heart from the dangers of pessimism, regret, hopelessness, and bitterness.

DAY 54

YOU'RE ACCOUNTABLE

But each person should examine his own work, and then he will have a reason for boasting in himself alone, and not in respect to someone else. For each person will have to carry his own load.

Galatians 6:4-5 HCSB

We humans are masters at passing the buck. Why? Because passing the buck is easier than fixing, and criticizing others is so much easier than improving ourselves. So instead of solving our problems legitimately (by doing the work required to solve them) we are inclined to fret, to blame, and to criticize, while doing precious little else. When we do, our problems, quite predictably, remain unsolved.

It's easy to hold other people accountable, but real accountability begins with the person in the mirror.

Whether you like it or not, you (and only you) are accountable for your actions. But because you are human, you'll be sorely tempted to pass the blame. Avoid that temptation at all costs.

Problem-solving builds character. Every time you straighten your back and look squarely into the face of Old Man Trouble, you'll strengthen not only your backbone but also your spirit. So, instead of looking for someone to blame, look for something to fix, and then get busy fixing it. And as you consider your own situation, remember this: God has a way of helping those who help themselves, but He doesn't spend much time helping those who don't.

FOOD FOR THOUGHT

Generally speaking, accountability is a willingness to share our activities, conduct, and fulfillment of assigned responsibilities with others.

Charles Stanley

Though I know intellectually how vulnerable I am to pride and power, I am the last one to know when I succumb to their seduction. That's why spiritual Lone Rangers are so dangerous—and why we must depend on trusted brothers and sisters who love us enough to tell us the truth.

Chuck Colson

STRENGTHENING YOUR FAITH

Accountability and character are traveling partners. If you want to build character, you need to assume responsibility for your actions. Once you begin to hold yourself accountable, you'll begin to grow emotionally and spiritually.

DAY 55

GOD'S PLAN FOR YOUR HEALTH

Who are those who fear the Lord? He will show them the path they should choose. They will live in prosperity, and their children will inherit the Promised Land.

Psalm 25:12-13 NLT

The journey toward improved health is not only a common-sense exercise in personal discipline, it is also a spiritual journey ordained by our Creator. God does not intend that we abuse our bodies by giving in to excessive appetites or to slothful behavior. To the contrary, God has instructed us to protect our physical bodies to the greatest extent we can. To do otherwise is to disobey Him.

God has a plan for your spiritual, physical, and emotional health.

When you make the decision to seek God's will for your life—and you should—then you will contemplate His Word, and you will be watchful for His signs. God intends to use you in wonderful, unexpected ways if you let Him. But be forewarned: the decision to seek God's plan and fulfill His purpose is ultimately a decision that you must make by yourself and for yourself. The consequences of that decision have implications that are both profound and eternal, so choose carefully. And then, as you go about your daily activities, keep your eyes and ears open, as well as your heart, because God is patiently trying to get His message through . . . and there's no better moment than this one for you to help Him.

FOOD FOR THOUGHT

God has a plan for the life of every Christian. Every circumstance, every turn of destiny, all things work together for your good and for His glory.

Billy Graham

But grow in the grace and knowledge of our Lord and Savior Jesus Christ. To Him be the glory both now and to the day of eternity.

2 Peter 3:18 HCSB

A HEALTHY-CHOICE TIP

We live in a junk-food society, but you shouldn't let your house become junk-food heaven. Make your home a haven of healthy foods. And remember, it's never too soon to teach your kid good habits . . . and that includes the very good habit of sensible eating.

DAY 56

BE A CHEERFUL CHRISTIAN

A cheerful heart has a continual feast.

Proverbs 15:15 HCSB

Few things in life are more sad, or, for that matter, more absurd, than a grumpy Christian. Christ promises us lives of abundance and joy, but He does not force His joy upon us. We must claim His joy for ourselves, and when we do, Jesus, in turn, fills our spirits with His power and His love.

How can we receive from Christ the joy that is rightfully ours? By giving Him what is rightfully His: our hearts and our souls.

When we earnestly commit ourselves to the Savior of mankind, and when we place Jesus at the center of our lives and trust Him as our personal Savior, He will transform us, not just for today, but for all eternity. Then we, as God's children, can share Christ's joy and His message with a world that needs both.

Cheerfulness is its own reward—but not its only reward.

FOOD FOR THOUGHT

Joy is the serious business of heaven.

C. S. Lewis

God is good, and heaven is forever. And if those two facts don't cheer you up, nothing will.

Marie T. Freeman

We may run, walk, stumble, drive, or fly, but let us never lose sight of the reason for the journey, or miss a chance to see a rainbow on the way.

Gloria Gaither

When we bring sunshine into the lives of others, we're warmed by it ourselves. When we spill a little happiness, it splashes on us.

Barbara Johnson

A HEALTHY-CHOICE TIP

God has given you many blessings, and you have many reasons to be cheerful. So what are you waiting for?

DAY 57

PERSPECTIVE AND BALANCE

Come to Me, all you who labor and are heavy laden, and I will give you rest. Take My yoke upon you and learn from Me, for I am gentle and lowly in heart, and you will find rest for your souls. For My yoke is easy and My burden is light.

Matthew 11:28-30 NKJV

Sometimes, amid the demands of daily life, we lose perspective. Life seems out of balance, and the pressures of everyday living seem overwhelming. What's needed is a fresh perspective, a restored sense of balance…and God.

Life is a balancing act. To improve your balance, consult your Heavenly Father many times each day.

If a temporary loss of perspective has robbed you of the spiritual fitness that should be yours in Christ, it's time to readjust your thought patterns. Negative thoughts are habit-forming; thankfully, so are positive ones. With practice, you can form the habit of focusing on God's priorities and your possibilities. When you do, you'll soon discover that you will spend less time fretting about your challenges and more time praising God for His gifts.

When you call upon the Lord and prayerfully seek His will, He will give you wisdom and perspective. When you make God's priorities your priorities, He will direct your steps and calm your fears. So today and every day hereafter, pray for a sense of balance and perspective. And remember: your thoughts are intensely powerful things, so handle them with care.

FOOD FOR THOUGHT

Prescription for a happier and healthier life: resolve to slow down your pace; learn to say no gracefully; resist the temptation to chase after more pleasure, more hobbies, and more social entanglements.

James Dobson

Work is not always required of a man. There is such a thing as sacred idleness, the cultivation of which is now fearfully neglected.

George MacDonald

A HEALTHY-CHOICE TIP

Need balance? Have a daily planning session with God. A regularly scheduled time of prayer, Bible reading, and meditation can help you prioritize your day and your life. And what if you're simply too busy to spend five or ten minutes with God? If so, it's time to reorder your priorities.

DAY 58

EMOTIONS: WHO'S IN CHARGE OF YOURS?

For this very reason, make every effort to supplement your faith with goodness, goodness with knowledge, knowledge with self-control, self-control with endurance, endurance with godliness.

2 Peter 1:5-6 HCSB

Hebrews 10:38 teaches us that, "The just shall live by faith." Yet sometimes, despite our best intentions, negative feelings can rob us of the peace and abundance that would otherwise be ours through Christ. When anger or anxiety separates us from the spiritual blessings that God has in store, we must rethink our priorities and renew our faith. And we must place faith above feelings. Human emotions are highly variable, decidedly unpredictable, and often unreliable. Our emotions are like the weather, only far more fickle. So we must learn to live by faith, not by the ups and downs of our own emotional roller coasters.

If you think you've lost control over your emotions, don't make big decisions, don't strike out against anybody, and don't speak out in anger.

Sometime during this day, you will probably be gripped by a strong negative emotion. Distrust it. Reign it in. Test it. And turn it over to God. Your emotions will inevitably change; God will not. So trust Him completely as you watch your feelings slowly evaporate into thin air—which, of course, they will.

FOOD FOR THOUGHT

Don't bother much about your feelings. When they are humble, loving, brave, give thanks for them; when they are conceited, selfish, cowardly, ask to have them altered. In neither case are they you, but only a thing that happens to you. What matters is your intentions and your behavior.

C. S. Lewis

I may no longer depend on pleasant impulses to bring me before the Lord. I must rather respond to principles I know to be right, whether I feel them to be enjoyable or not.

Jim Elliot

A HEALTHY-CHOICE TIP

Fitness is a journey, not a destination. Achieving physical fitness and maintaining it is a seven-day-a-week assignment. If you don't make physical fitness a priority, your health will suffer.

DAY 59

BEYOND EXCUSES

Let us walk with decency, as in the daylight: not in carousing and drunkenness.

Romans 13:13 HCSB

All too often we are quick to proclaim ourselves "victims," and we refuse to take responsibility for our actions. So we make excuses, excuses, and more excuses—with predictably poor results.

Today, think of something important that you've been putting off. Then, ask yourself what you can do today to finish the work you've been avoiding.

We live in a world where excuses are everywhere. And it's precisely because excuses are so numerous that they are also so ineffective. When we hear the words, "I'm sorry but...," most of us know exactly what is to follow: the excuse. The dog ate the homework. Traffic was terrible. It's the company's fault. The boss is to blame. The equipment is broken. We're out of that. And so forth, and so on.

Because we humans are such creative excuse-makers, all of the really good excuses have already been taken. In fact, the high-quality excuses have been used, re-used, over-used, and abused. That's why excuses don't work—we've heard them all before.

So, if you're wasting your time trying to portray yourself as a victim (and weakening your character in the process), or if you're trying to concoct a new and improved excuse, don't bother. Excuses don't work, and while you're inventing them, neither do you.

FOOD FOR THOUGHT

Replace your excuses with fresh determination.

Charles Swindoll

If you're looking for an excuse, you probably won't have much trouble finding it.

Criswell Freeman

An excuse is only the skin of a reason stuffed with a lie.

Vance Havner

A HEALTHY-CHOICE TIP

If you're genuinely planning on becoming a disciplined person "some day" in the distant future, you're deluding yourself. The best day to begin exercising self-discipline is this one.

DAY 60

BE STILL

Be still, and know that I am God.

Psalm 46:10 NKJV

In the first chapter of Mark, we read that in the darkness of the early morning hours, Jesus went to a solitary place and prayed. So, too, should we. But sometimes, finding quiet moments of solitude is difficult indeed.

We live in a noisy world, a world filled with distractions, frustrations, and complications. But if we allow the distractions of a clamorous world to separate us from God's peace, we do ourselves a profound disservice.

Be still and listen to God. He has something important to say to you.

If we seek to maintain righteous minds and compassionate hearts, we must take time each day for prayer and for meditation. We must make ourselves still in the presence of our Creator. We must quiet our minds and our hearts so that we can sense God's will, God's love, and God's Son.

Are you one of those busy men who rushes through the day with scarcely a single moment for quiet contemplation and prayer? If so, it's time to reorder your priorities.

Has the busy pace of life robbed you of the peace that might otherwise be yours through Jesus Christ? Nothing is more important than the time you spend with your Savior. So be still and claim the inner peace that is your spiritual birthright: the peace of Jesus Christ. It is offered freely; it has been paid for in full; it is yours for the asking. So ask. And then share.

FOOD FOR THOUGHT

If you, too, will learn to wait upon God, to get alone with Him, and remain silent so that you can hear His voice when He is ready to speak to you, what a difference it will make in your life!

Kay Arthur

A HEALTHY-CHOICE TIP

In the good old days, dining out used to be an occasional treat for most families. Now, it's more of an everyday occurrence. But there's a catch: most restaurants aim for taste first, price second, and health a distant third. But you should think health first. So the next time you head out for a burger, a bagel, or any other fast food, take a minute to read the fine print that's usually posted on the wall. You may find out that the healthy-sounding treat is actually a calorie-bomb in disguise.

DAY 61

ACCEPTING LIFE

Do not remember the past events, pay no attention to things of old. Look, I am about to do something new; even now it is coming. Do you not see it? Indeed, I will make a way in the wilderness, rivers in the desert.

Isaiah 43:18-19 HCSB

If you're like most people, you like being in control. Period. When you're trying to improve your health—or any other aspect of your life, for that matter—you want things to happen in accordance with your own specific timetable. But sometimes, God has other plans . . . and He always has the final word.

Think of at least one aspect of your life that you've been reluctant to accept, and then ask God to help you with it.

All of us experience adversity and pain. As human beings with limited comprehension, we can never fully understand the will of our Father in Heaven. But as believers in a benevolent God, we must always trust His providence.

When Jesus went to the Mount of Olives, as described in Luke 22, He poured out His heart to God. Jesus knew of the agony that He was destined to endure, but He also knew that God's will must be done. We, like our Savior, face trials that bring fear and trembling to the very depths of our souls, but like Christ, we too must ultimately seek God's will, not our own.

Are you embittered by a personal tragedy that you did not deserve and cannot understand? If so, it's time to make peace with life. It's time to forgive others, and, if necessary, to forgive yourself. It's time to accept the unchangeable past, to embrace the priceless present, and to have faith in the promise of tomorrow. It's time to trust God completely. And it's time to reclaim the peace—His peace—that can and should be yours.

FOOD FOR THOUGHT

Prayer may not get us what we want, but it will teach us to want what we need.

Vance Havner

I am truly grateful that faith enables me to move past the question of "Why?"

Zig Ziglar

A HEALTHY-CHOICE TIP

Here's a time-tested formula for success: have faith in God and do the work. It has been said that there are no shortcuts to any place worth going, and those words apply to your physical fitness, too. There are simply no shortcuts to a healthy lifestyle.

DAY 62

RECHARGING YOUR SPIRITUAL BATTERIES

Those who hope in the LORD will renew their strength. They will soar on wings like eagles; they will run and not grow weary, they will walk and not be faint.

Isaiah 40:31 NIV

As you make the journey toward improved fitness, you'll undoubtedly run out of energy from time to time. When it happens, you can turn to God for strength and for guidance.

Andrew Murray observed, "Where there is much prayer, there will be much of the Spirit; where there is much of the Spirit, there will be ever-increasing power." These words remind us that the ultimate source of our strength is God. When we turn to Him—for guidance, for enlightenment, and for strength—we will not be disappointed.

For the journey through life, you need energy. The best source of energy, of course, is God. Ask the Creator to energize you and guide you every day.

Are you feeling exhausted? Are your emotions on edge? If so, it's time to turn things over to God in prayer. Are you weak or worried? Take the time—or, more accurately, make the time—to delve deeply into God's Holy

Word. Are you spiritually depleted? Call upon fellow believers to support you, and call upon Christ to renew your spirit and your life. When you do, you'll discover that the Creator of the universe has the power to make all things new . . . including you.

FOOD FOR THOUGHT

Jesus taught us by example to get out of the rat race and recharge our batteries.

Barbara Johnson

Troubles we bear trustfully can bring us a fresh vision of God and a new outlook on life, an outlook of peace and hope.

Billy Graham

God allows us to experience the low points of life in order to teach us lessons that we could learn in no other way.

C. S. Lewis

A HEALTHY-CHOICE TIP

God wants you to experience abundant life, but He will not force you to adopt a healthy lifestyle. Managing your food and your fitness is up to you.

DAY 63

MODERATION IS WISDOM IN ACTION

Now if any of you lacks wisdom, he should ask God, who gives to all generously and without criticizing, and it will be given to him.

James 1:5 HCSB

Moderation and wisdom are traveling companions. If we are wise, we must learn to temper our appetites, our desires, and our impulses. When we do, we are blessed, in part, because God has created a world in which temperance is rewarded and intemperance is inevitably punished.

Moderation pays.
Excess doesn't.
Behave accordingly.

When we allow our appetites to run wild, they usually do. When we abandon moderation, we forfeit the inner peace that God offers—but does not guarantee—to His children. When we live intemperate lives, we rob ourselves of countless blessings that would have otherwise been ours.

God's instructions are clear: if we seek to live wisely, we must be moderate in our appetites and disciplined in our behavior. To do otherwise is an affront to Him . . . and to ourselves.

FOOD FOR THOUGHT

Teach me, O Lord, the way of Your statutes, and I shall keep it to the end.

Psalm 119:33 NKJV

So teach us to number our days, that we may gain a heart of wisdom.

Psalm 90:12 NKJV

Acquire wisdom—how much better it is than gold! And acquire understanding—it is preferable to silver.

Proverbs 16:16 HCSB

A HEALTHY-CHOICE TIP

Of a thousand American adults who were surveyed in a recent poll, eighty-eight percent were unable to accurately estimate how many calories they should consume each day to maintain their weight. Consequently, these adults didn't know how many calories they should consume if they wanted to lose weight. Thankfully, in these days of easy Internet information, it isn't very difficult to discover how many calories you need. So do the research and find your calorie target. Then, aim for the bull's-eye that leads to better health and a longer life.

DAY 64

BEYOND COMPLAINING

Be hospitable to one another without complaining.

1 Peter 4:9 HCSB

Most of us have more blessings than we can count, yet we can still find reasons to complain about the minor frustrations of everyday life. To do so, of course, is not only shortsighted, but it is also a serious roadblock on the path to spiritual abundance.

Would you like to feel more comfortable about your circumstances and your life? Then promise yourself that you'll do whatever it takes to ensure that you focus your thoughts and energy on the major blessings you've received (not the minor inconveniences you must occasionally endure).

> If you're wise, you'll fill your heart with gratitude. When you do, there's simply no room left for complaints.

So the next time you're tempted to complain about the inevitable frustrations of everyday living, don't do it! Today and every day, make it a practice to count your blessings, not your hardships. It's the truly decent way to live.

FOOD FOR THOUGHT

I am sure it is never sadness—a proper, straight, natural response to loss—that does people harm, but all the other things, all the resentment, dismay, doubt and self-pity with which it is usually complicated.

C. S. Lewis

When you're on the verge of throwing a pity party thanks to your despairing thoughts, go back to the Word of God.

Charles Swindoll

It's your choice: you can either count your blessings or recount your disappointments.

Jim Gallery

He wants us to have a faith that does not complain while waiting, but rejoices because we know our times are in His hands—nail-scarred hands that labor for our highest good.

Kay Arthur

A HEALTHY-CHOICE TIP

If you're wise, you'll try to spend more time counting your blessings and less time counting your problems.

DAY 65

YOU AND YOUR CONSCIENCE

Blessed is the man who does not condemn himself.

Romans 14:22 HCSB

Billy Graham correctly observed, "Most of us follow our conscience as we follow a wheelbarrow. We push it in front of us in the direction we want to go." To do so, of course, is a profound mistake. Yet all of us, on occasion, have failed to listen to the voice that God planted in our hearts, and all of us have suffered the consequences of our choices.

Listen carefully to your conscience. That little voice inside your head will seldom lead you astray.

God gave each of us a conscience for a very good reason: to listen to it. Wise believers make it a practice to listen carefully to that quiet internal voice. Count yourself among that number. When your conscience speaks, listen and learn. In all likelihood, God is trying to get His message through. And in all likelihood, it is a message that you desperately need to hear.

Few things in life torment us more than a guilty conscience. And, few things in life provide more contentment than the knowledge that we are obeying God's commandments. A clear conscience is one of the rewards we earn when we obey God's Word and follow His will. When we follow God's will and accept His gift of salvation, our earthly rewards are never-ceasing, and our heavenly rewards are everlasting.

FOOD FOR THOUGHT

To go against one's conscience is neither safe nor right. Here I stand. I cannot do otherwise.

Martin Luther

A quiet conscience sleeps in thunder.

Thomas Fuller

He that loses his conscience has nothing left that is worth keeping.

Izaak Walton

A HEALTHY-CHOICE TIP

Are you chained to a desk or trapped in a sedentary lifestyle? And are you waiting for something big to happen before you revolutionize your exercise habits? If so, wait no more. In fact, you can start today by substituting a light snack and a healthy walk for that calorie-laden lunch.

DAY 66

TRUSTING HIS PROMISES

Let us hold on to the confession of our hope without wavering, for He who promised is faithful.

Hebrews 10:23 HCSB

What do you expect from the day ahead? Are you willing to trust God completely, or are you living beneath a cloud of doubt and fear? God's Word makes it clear: you should trust Him and His promises, and when you do, you can live courageously.

For thoughtful Christians, every day begins and ends with God's Son and God's promises. When we accept Christ into our hearts, God promises us the opportunity for earthly peace and spiritual abundance. But more importantly, God promises us the priceless gift of eternal life.

Sometimes, especially when we find ourselves caught in the inevitable entanglements of life, we fail to trust God completely.

God has made many promises to you, and He will keep every single one of them. Your job is to trust God's promises and live accordingly.

Are you tired? Discouraged? Fearful? Be comforted and trust the promises that God has made to you. Are you worried or anxious? Be confident in God's power. Do you see a difficult future ahead? Be courageous and call upon God.

He will protect you and then use you according to His purposes. Are you confused? Listen to the quiet voice of your Heavenly Father. He is not a God of confusion. Talk with Him; listen to Him; trust Him, and trust His promises. He is steadfast, and He is your Protector . . . forever.

FOOD FOR THOUGHT

There are four words I wish we would never forget, and they are, "God keeps his word."

Charles Swindoll

The stars may fall, but God's promises will stand and be fulfilled.

J. I. Packer

We honor God by asking for great things when they are a part of His promise. We dishonor Him and cheat ourselves when we ask for molehills where He has promised mountains.

Vance Havner

STRENGTHENING YOUR FAITH

Of this you can be sure: God's faithfulness is steadfast, unwavering, and eternal.

DAY 67

HE IS SUFFICIENT

And He said to me, "My grace is sufficient for you, for My strength is made perfect in weakness."

2 Corinthians 12:9 NKJV

Of this you can be certain: God is sufficient to meet your needs. Period.

Do the demands of life seem overwhelming at times? If so, you must learn to rely not only upon your own resources, but also upon the promises of your Father in heaven. God will hold your hand and walk with you and your family if you let Him. So even if your circumstances are difficult, trust the Father.

The Psalmist writes, "Weeping may endure for a night, but joy comes in the morning" (Psalm 30:5 NKJV). But when we are suffering, the morning may seem very far away. It is not. God promises that He is "near to those who have a broken heart" (Psalm 34:18 NKJV). When we are troubled, we must turn to Him, and we must encourage our friends and family members to do likewise.

If you'd like infinite protection, there's only one place you can receive it: from an infinite God.

If you are discouraged by the inevitable demands of life here on earth, be mindful of this fact: the loving heart of God is sufficient to meet any challenge.

FOOD FOR THOUGHT

Jesus has been consistently affectionate and true to us. He has shared his great wealth with us. How can we doubt the all-powerful, all-sufficient Lord?

C. H. Spurgeon

God's saints in all ages have realized that God was enough for them. God is enough for time; God is enough for eternity. God is enough!

Hannah Whitall Smith

God will call you to obey Him and do whatever he asks of you. However, you do not need to be doing something to feel fulfilled. You are fulfilled completely in a relationship with God. When you are filled with Him, what else do you need?

Henry Blackaby and Claude King

Yes, God's grace is always sufficient, and His arms are always open to give it. But, will our arms be open to receive it?

Beth Moore

STRENGTHENING YOUR FAITH

Whatever you need, God can provide. He is always sufficient to meet your needs.

DAY 68

STUDYING HIS WORD

Man shall not live by bread alone, but by every word that proceeds from the mouth of God.

Matthew 4:4 NKJV

Is Bible study a high priority for you? The answer to this simple question will determine, to a surprising extent, the quality of your life and the direction of your faith.

As you establish priorities for life, you must decide whether God's Word will be a bright spotlight that guides your path every day or a tiny nightlight that occasionally flickers in the dark. The decision to study the Bible—or not—is yours and yours alone. But make no mistake: how you choose to use your Bible will have a profound impact on you and your loved ones.

Today, think carefully about the role that the Bible plays in your everyday life.

George Mueller observed, "The vigor of our spiritual lives will be in exact proportion to the place held by the Bible in our lives and in our thoughts." Think of it like this: the more you use your Bible, the more God will use you.

Perhaps you're one of those Christians who owns a bookshelf full of unread Bibles. If so, remember the old saying, "A Bible in the hand is worth two in the bookcase." Or perhaps you're one of those folks who is simply "too busy" to find time for a daily dose of prayer and Bible study. If so, remember the old adage, "It's hard to stumble when you're on your knees."

God's Word can be a roadmap to a place of righteousness and abundance. Make it your roadmap. God's wisdom can be a light to guide your steps. Claim it as your light today, tomorrow, and every day of your life—and then walk confidently in the footsteps of God's only begotten Son.

FOOD FOR THOUGHT

Nobody ever outgrows Scripture; the book widens and deepens with our years.

C. H. Spurgeon

Only through routine, regular exposure to God's Word can you and I draw out the nutrition needed to grow a heart of faith.

Elizabeth George

STRENGTHENING YOUR FAITH

Even if you've been studying the Bible for many years, you've still got lots to learn. Bible study should be a lifelong endeavor; make it your lifelong endeavor.

DAY 69

SMALL STEPS

So we must not get tired of doing good, for we will reap at the proper time if we don't give up.

Galatians 6:9 HCSB

If you want to become more physically fit, you don't have to make one giant leap. You can start with many small steps, and you should. When it comes to any new exercise regimen, starting slowly and improving gradually is the smart way to do it.

Crash diets usually crash. And fitness fads fade. But sensible exercise, when combined with a moderate diet, produces results that last.

So if you're determined to improve the state of your health, remember that consistency is the key. Start slowly, avoid injury, be consistent, and expect gradual improvement, not instant success.

Today, think of one or two small steps you can take to improve your physical and spiritual health.

FOOD FOR THOUGHT

Do you not know that the runners in a stadium all race, but only one receives the prize? Run in such a way that you may win. Now everyone who competes exercises self-control in everything. However, they do it to receive a perishable crown, but we an imperishable one.

1 Corinthians 9:24-25 HCSB

It is better to finish something than to start it. It is better to be patient than to be proud.

Ecclesiastes 7:8 NCV

Battles are won in the trenches, in the grit and grime of courageous determination; they are won day by day in the arena of life.

Charles Swindoll

By perseverance the snail reached the ark.

C. H. *Spurgeon*

A HEALTHY-CHOICE TIP

Becoming fit—and staying fit—is an exercise in perseverance. If you give up at the first sign of trouble, you won't accomplish much. But if you don't give up, you'll eventually improve your health and your life.

DAY 70

ACCEPTING GOD'S CALLING

But as God has distributed to each one, as the Lord has called each one, so let him walk.

1 Corinthians 7:17 NKJV

God is calling you to follow a specific path that He has chosen for your life. And it is vitally important that you heed that call. Otherwise, your talents and opportunities may go unused.

Have you already heard God's call? And are you pursuing it with vigor? If so, you're both fortunate and wise. But if you have not yet discovered what God intends for you to do with your life, keep searching and keep praying until you discover why the Creator put you here.

Remember: God has important work for you to do—work that no one else on earth can accomplish but you. The Creator has placed you in a particular location, amid particular people, with unique opportunities to serve. And He has given you all the tools you need to succeed. So listen for His voice, watch for His signs, and prepare yourself for the call that is sure to come.

God has a plan for your life, a divine calling that you can either answer or ignore. Your choice to respond to it will determine the direction you take and the contributions you make.

FOOD FOR THOUGHT

When you become consumed by God's call on your life, everything will take on new meaning and significance. You will begin to see every facet of your life, including your pain, as a means through which God can work to bring others to Himself.

Charles Stanley

If God has called you, do not spend time looking over your shoulder to see who is following you.

Corrie ten Boom

God tends to lead us through gentle spiritual promptings.

Bill Hybels

God's help is near and always available, but it is only given to those who seek it.

Max Lucado

A HEALTHY-CHOICE TIP

Physical fitness is not the result of a single decision that is made "once and for all." Physical fitness results from thousands of decisions that are made day after day, week after week, and year after year.

DAY 71

THE SOURCE OF STRENGTH

And He said to me, "My grace is sufficient for you, for My strength is made perfect in weakness."

2 Corinthians 12:9 NKJV

Where do you go to find strength? The gym? The health food store? The espresso bar? There's a better source of strength, of course, and that source is God. He is a never-ending source of strength and courage if you call upon Him.

Today, think about ways that you can tap into God's strength: try prayer, worship, and praise, for starters.

Are you an energized Christian? You should be. But if you're not, you must seek strength and renewal from the source that will never fail: that source, of course, is your Heavenly Father. And rest assured—when you sincerely petition Him, He will give you all the strength you need to live victoriously for Him.

Have you "tapped in" to the power of God? Have you turned your life and your heart over to Him, or are you muddling along under your own power? The answer to this question will determine the quality of your life here on earth and the destiny of your life throughout all eternity. So start tapping in—and remember that when it comes to strength, God is the Ultimate Source.

FOOD FOR THOUGHT

The God we seek is a God who is intrinsically righteous and who will be so forever. With His example and His strength, we can share in that righteousness.

Bill Hybels

By ourselves we are not capable of suffering bravely, but the Lord possesses all the strength we lack and will demonstrate His power when we undergo persecution.

Corrie ten Boom

Cast yourself into the arms of God and be very sure that if He wants anything of you, He will fit you for the work and give you strength.

Philip Neri

A HEALTHY-CHOICE TIP

As you petition God each morning, ask Him for the strength and the wisdom to treat your body as His creation and His "temple." During the day ahead, you will face countless temptations to do otherwise, but with God's help, you can treat your body as the priceless, one-of-a-kind gift that it most certainly is.

DAY 72

REBELLION INVITES DISASTER

You must follow the Lord your God and fear Him. You must keep His commands and listen to His voice; you must worship Him and remain faithful to Him.

Deuteronomy 13:4 HCSB

For most of us, it is a daunting thought: one day, perhaps soon, we'll come face to face with our Heavenly Father, and we'll be called to account for our actions here on earth. Our personal histories will certainly not be surprising to God; He already knows everything about us. But the full scope of our activities may be surprising to us: some of us will be pleasantly surprised; others will not be.

Obedience is the outward expression of your love of God.

Henry Blackaby

God's commandments are not offered as helpful hints or timely tips. God's commandments are not suggestions; they are ironclad rules for living, rules that we disobey at our own risk.

The English clergyman Thomas Fuller observed, "He does not believe who does not live according to his beliefs." These words are most certainly true. We may proclaim our beliefs to our hearts' content, but our proclamations will mean nothing—to others or to ourselves—unless we accompany our words with deeds that match. The sermons that we live are far more compelling than the ones we preach.

So today, do whatever you can to ensure that your thoughts and your deeds are pleasing to your Creator. Because you will, at some point in the future, be called to account for your actions. And the future may be sooner than you think.

FOOD FOR THOUGHT

The Fall is simply and solely Disobedience—doing what you have been told not to do: and it results from Pride—from being too big for your boots, forgetting your place, thinking that you are God.

C. S. *Lewis*

Only he who believes is obedient, and only he who is obedient believes.

Dietrich Bonhoeffer

STRENGTHENING YOUR FAITH

Every day of your life, you will be tempted to rebel against God's teachings. Your job, simply put, is to guard your heart against the darkness as you focus on the light.

DAY 73

HOLDING ON TO HOPE

We have this hope—like a sure and firm anchor of the soul—that enters the inner sanctuary behind the curtain.

Hebrews 6:19 HCSB

There are few sadder sights on earth than the sight of a man or woman who has lost all hope. In difficult times, hope can be elusive, but those who place their faith in God's promises need never lose it. After all, God is good; His love endures; He has promised His children the gift of eternal life. And, God keeps His promises.

If you're experiencing hard times, you'll be wise to start spending more time with God. Never be afraid to hope—or to ask—for a miracle.

Despite God's promises, despite Christ's love, and despite our countless blessings, we frail human beings can still lose hope from time to time. When we do, we need the encouragement of Christian friends, the life-changing power of prayer, and the healing truth of God's Holy Word.

If you find yourself falling into the spiritual traps of worry and discouragement, seek the healing touch of Jesus and the encouraging words of fellow Christians. If you find a friend in need, remind him or her of the peace that is found through a personal relationship with Christ. It was

Christ who promised, "These things I have spoken unto you, that in me ye might have peace. In the world ye shall have tribulation: but be of good cheer; I have overcome the world" (John 16:33 KJV). This world can be a place of trials and tribulations, but as believers, we are secure. God has promised us peace, joy, and eternal life. And, of course, God keeps His promises today, tomorrow, and forever.

FOOD FOR THOUGHT

Faith looks back and draws courage; hope looks ahead and keeps desire alive.

John Eldredge

If your hopes are being disappointed just now, it means that they are being purified.

Oswald Chambers

A HEALTHY-CHOICE TIP

If you genuinely want to exercise more, find exercise that you enjoy. And if you can't seem to find exercise that you enjoy, search for ways to make your current exercise program a little less painful and a little more fun.

DAY 74

THE GIFT OF GOD'S GRACE

But God, who is abundant in mercy, because of His great love that He had for us, made us alive with the Messiah even though we were dead in trespasses. By grace you are saved!

Ephesians 2:4-5 HCSB

We have received countless gifts from God, but none can compare with the gift of salvation. When we accept Christ into our hearts, we are saved by God's grace. The familiar words of Ephesians 2:8 make God's promise perfectly clear: we are saved, not by our actions, but by God's mercy. We are saved, not because of our good deeds, but because of our faith in Christ.

God's grace isn't earned, but freely given—what an amazing, humbling gift.

God's grace is the ultimate gift, and we owe Him the ultimate in thanksgiving. Let us praise the Creator for His priceless gift, and let us share the Good News with all who cross our paths. We return our Father's love by accepting His grace and by sharing His message and His love. When we do, we are blessed here on earth and throughout all eternity.

FOOD FOR THOUGHT

The grace of God is sufficient for all our needs, for every problem, and for every difficulty, for every broken heart, and for every human sorrow.

Peter Marshall

To believe is to take freely what God gives freely.

C. H. Spurgeon

Number one, God brought me here. It is by His will that I am in this place. In that fact I will rest. Number two, He will keep me here in His love and give me grace to behave as His child. Number three, He will make the trial a blessing, teaching me the lessons He intends for me to learn and working in me the grace He means to bestow. Number four, in His good time He can bring me out again. How and when, He knows. So, let me say I am here.

Andrew Murray

A HEALTHY-CHOICE TIP

If someone else is cooking your meals, ask that person to help you plan a healthier diet. Without the cooperation of the person who cooks your food, you'll have an incredibly difficult time sticking to a healthier diet.

DAY 75

LEARNING WHEN TO SAY NO

So let us run the race that is before us and never give up. We should remove from our lives anything that would get in the way and the sin that so easily holds us back.

Hebrews 12:1 NCV

You live in a busy world, a world where many folks may be making demands upon your time. If you're like most men, you've got plenty of people pulling you in lots of directions, starting, of course, with your family—but not ending there.

You have a right to say no. Don't feel guilty about asserting that right.

Perhaps you also have additional responsibilities at work or at church. Maybe you're active in community affairs, or maybe you involved in any of a hundred other activities that gobble up big portions of your day. If so, you'll need to be sure that you know when to say enough is enough.

When it comes to squeezing more and more obligations onto your daily to-do list, you have the right to say no when you simply don't have the time, the energy, or the desire to do the job. And if you're wise, you'll learn so say no as often as necessary . . . or else!

FOOD FOR THOUGHT

Prescription for a happier and healthier life: resolve to slow down your pace; learn to say no gracefully; resist the temptation to chase after more pleasure, more hobbies, and more social entanglements.

James Dobson

Judge everything in the light of Jesus Christ.

Oswald Chambers

Life is built on character, but character is built on decisions.

Warren Wiersbe

Great relief and satisfaction can come from seeking God's priorities for us in each season, discerning what is "best" in the midst of many noble opportunities, and pouring our most excellent energies into those things.

Beth Moore

A HEALTHY-CHOICE TIP

In a world where rich foods and high-calorie treats are both cheap and plentiful, it's wise to learn how to say no to your taste buds. When you say no to unhealthy foods, you're saying yes to better health.

DAY 76

THE GIFT OF LIFE

What a gift life is to those who stay the course! You've heard, of course, of Job's staying power, and you know how God brought it all together for him at the end. That's because God cares, cares right down to the last detail.

James 5:11 MSG

Life is a glorious gift from God. Treat it that way.

This day, like every other, is filled to the brim with opportunities, challenges, and choices. But, no choice that you make is more important than the choice you make concerning God. Today, you will either place Him at the center of your life—or not—and the consequences of that choice have implications that are both temporal and eternal.

Your life is a priceless opportunity, a gift of incalculable worth. You should thank God for the gift of life.

Sometimes, we don't intentionally neglect God; we simply allow ourselves to become overwhelmed with the demands of everyday life. And then, without our even realizing it, we gradually drift away from the One we need most. Thankfully, God never drifts away from us. He remains always present, always steadfast, always loving.

As you begin this day, place God and His Son where they belong: in your head, in your prayers, on your lips, and in your heart. And then, with God as your guide and companion, let the journey begin.

FOOD FOR THOUGHT

Jesus wants Life for us, Life with a capital L.

John Eldredge

Our Lord is the Bread of Life. His proportions are perfect. There never was too much or too little of anything about Him. Feed on Him for a well-balanced ration. All the vitamins and calories are there.

Vance Havner

I have come that they may have life, and that they may have it more abundantly.

John 10:10 NKJV

STRENGTHENING YOUR FAITH

Life is a priceless gift from God. Spend time each day thanking God for His gift.

DAY 77

THE POWER OF PATIENCE

Be gentle to everyone, able to teach, and patient.

2 Timothy 2:23 HCSB

The dictionary defines the word patience as "the ability to be calm, tolerant, and understanding." If that describes you, you can skip the rest of this page. But, if you're like most of us, you'd better keep reading.

The best things in life seldom happen overnight; they usually take time.

For most of us, patience is a hard thing to master. Why? Because we have lots of things we want, and we know precisely when we want them: NOW (if not sooner). But our Father in heaven has other ideas; the Bible teaches that we must learn to wait patiently for the things that God has in store for us, even when waiting is difficult.

We live in an imperfect world inhabited by imperfect people. Sometimes, we inherit troubles from others, and sometimes we create troubles for ourselves. On other occasions, we see other people "moving ahead" in the world, and we want to move ahead with them. So we become impatient with ourselves, with our circumstances, and even with our Creator.

Psalm 37:7 commands us to "rest in the Lord, and wait patiently for Him" (NKJV). But, for most of us, waiting patiently for Him is hard. We are fallible human beings who seek solutions to our problems today, not tomorrow. Still, God instructs us to wait patiently for His plans to unfold, and that's exactly what we should do.

Sometimes, patience is the price we pay for being responsible adults, and that's as it should be. After all, think about how patient our Heavenly Father has been with us. So the next time you find yourself drumming your fingers as you wait for a quick resolution to the challenges of everyday living, take a deep breath and ask God for patience. Remember that patience builds character . . . and the best moment to start building is this one.

FOOD FOR THOUGHT

You can't step in front of God and not get in trouble. When He says, "Go three steps," don't go four.

Charles Stanley

A HEALTHY-CHOICE TIP

Every step of your life's journey is a choice . . . and the quality of those choices determines the quality of the journey.

DAY 78

THE POWER OF OPTIMISM

I am able to do all things through Him who strengthens me.

Philippians 4:13 HCSB

As each day unfolds, you are quite literally surrounded by more opportunities than you can count—opportunities to improve your own life and the lives of those you love. God's Word promises that you, like all of His children, possess the ability to experience earthly peace and spiritual abundance. Yet sometimes—especially if you dwell upon the inevitable disappointments that may, at times, befall even the luckiest among us—you may allow pessimism to invade your thoughts and your heart.

Be a realistic optimist. Think realistically about yourself and your situation while making a conscious effort to focus on hopes, not fears.

The self-fulfilling prophecy is alive, well, and living at your house. If you constantly anticipate the worst, that's what you're likely to attract. But, if you make the effort to think positive thoughts, you'll increase the probability that those positive thoughts will come true.

So here's a simple, character-building tip for improving your life: put the self-fulfilling prophecy to work for you. Expect the best, and then get busy working to achieve it.

When you do, you'll not only increase the odds of achieving your dreams, but you'll also have more fun along the way.

FOOD FOR THOUGHT

The popular idea of faith is of a certain obstinate optimism: the hope, tenaciously held in the face of trouble, that the universe is fundamentally friendly and things may get better.

J. I. Packer

The essence of optimism is that it takes no account of the present, but it is a source of inspiration, of vitality, and of hope. Where others have resigned, it enables a man to hold his head high, to claim the future for himself, and not abandon it to his enemy.

Dietrich Bonhoeffer

A HEALTHY-CHOICE TIP

Learn to look for opportunities, not obstructions; and while you're at it, look for possibilities, not problems.

DAY 79

CONTAGIOUS CHRISTIANITY

We are therefore Christ's ambassadors, as though God were making his appeal through us. We implore you on Christ's behalf: Be reconciled to God.

2 Corinthians 5:20 NIV

Genuine, heartfelt Christianity can be highly contagious. When you've experienced the transforming power of God's love, you feel the need to share the Good News of His only begotten Son. So, whether you realize it or not, you can be sure that you are being led to share the story of your faith with family, with friends, and with the world.

If you want to be more like Jesus . . . follow in His footsteps every day.

Every believer, including you, bears responsibility for sharing God's Good News. And it is important to remember that you share your testimony through words and actions, but not necessarily in that order.

Today, don't be bashful or timid: Talk about Jesus and, while you're at it, show the world what it really means to follow Him. After all, the fields are ripe for the harvest, time is short, and the workers are surprisingly few. So please share your story today because tomorrow may indeed be too late.

FOOD FOR THOUGHT

No man ever loved like Jesus. He taught the blind to see and the dumb to speak. He died on the cross to save us. He bore our sins. And now God says, "Because He did, I can forgive you."

Billy Graham

The richest meaning of your life is contained in the idea that Christ loved you enough to give His life for you.

Calvin Miller

Were the whole realm of nature mine, That were a present far too small: / Love so amazing, so divine, / Demands my soul, my life, my all.

Isaac Watts

A HEALTHY-CHOICE TIP

Take a careful look inside your refrigerator. Are the contents reflective of a healthy lifestyle? And if your fridge is overflowing with junk foods, it's time to rethink your shopping habits.

DAY 80

BUILD THE CHURCH OF GOD

Be on guard for yourselves and for all the flock, among whom the Holy Spirit has appointed you as overseers, to shepherd the church of God, which He purchased with His own blood.

Acts 20:28 HCSB

If you want to start building a healthier, happier life, the church is a wonderful place to do it. Are you an active, contributing, member of your local fellowship? The answer to this simple question will have a profound impact on the direction of your spiritual journey and the content of your character.

God intends for you to be actively involved in His church. Your intentions should be the same.

If you are not currently engaged in a local church, you're missing out on an array of blessings that include, but are certainly not limited to, the life-lifting relationships that you can—and should—be experiencing with fellow believers.

So do yourself a favor: Find a congregation you're comfortable with, and join it. And once you've joined, don't just attend church out of habit. Go to church out of a sincere desire to know and worship God. When you do, you'll be blessed by the men and women who attend your fellowship, and you'll be blessed by your Creator. You deserve to attend church, and God deserves for you to attend church, so don't delay.

FOOD FOR THOUGHT

The church is where it's at. The first place of Christian service for any Christian is in a local church.

Jerry Clower

What the church needs is not better machinery nor new organizations, but instead it needs men whom the Holy Spirit can use—men of prayer, men mighty in prayer.

E. M. Bounds

To model the kingdom of God in the world, the church must not only be a repentant community, committed to truth, but also a holy community.

Chuck Colson

STRENGTHENING YOUR FAITH

Make church a celebration, not an obligation: What you put into church determines what you get out of it. Your attitude towards worship is vitally important . . . so celebrate accordingly!

DAY 81

DURING DIFFICULT DAYS

We also have joy with our troubles, because we know that these troubles produce patience. And patience produces character, and character produces hope.

Romans 5:3-4 NCV

All of us face those occasional days when the traffic jams and the dog gobbles the homework. But, when we find ourselves overtaken by the minor frustrations of life, we must catch ourselves, take a deep breath, and lift our thoughts upward. Although we are here on earth struggling to rise above the distractions of the day, we need never struggle alone. God is here—eternally and faithfully, with infinite patience and love—and, if we reach out to Him, He will restore perspective and peace to our souls.

Difficult days come and go. Stay the course. The sun is shining somewhere, and will soon shine on you.

Sometimes even the most devout Christians can become discouraged, and you are no exception. After all, you live in a world where expectations can be high and demands can be even higher.

If you find yourself enduring difficult circumstances, remember that God remains in His heaven. If you become discouraged with the direction of your day or your life, lift your thoughts and prayers to Him. He is a God of possibility, not negativity. He will guide you through your difficulties and beyond them. Then, you can thank the Giver of all things good for blessings that are simply too numerous to count.

FOOD FOR THOUGHT

Our Heavenly Father never takes anything from his children unless he means to give them something better.

George Mueller

There is a world of difference between a person who has a big problem and a person who makes a problem big.

John Maxwell

A HEALTHY-CHOICE TIP

Many of the messages that you receive from the media are specifically designed to sell you products that interfere with your spiritual, physical, or emotional health. God takes great interest in your health; the moguls from Madison Avenue take great interest in your pocketbook. Trust God.

DAY 82

LASTING PEACE

Be of good comfort, be of one mind, live in peace; and the God of love and peace will be with you.

2 Corinthians 13:11 NKJV

Have you found the lasting peace that can—and should—be yours through Jesus Christ? Or are you still chasing the illusion of "peace and happiness" that the world promises but cannot deliver?

The beautiful words of John 14:27 promise that Jesus offers peace, not as the world gives, but as He alone gives: "Peace I leave with you. My peace I give to you. I do not give to you as the world gives. Your heart must not be troubled or fearful" (HCSB). Your challenge is to accept Christ's peace into your heart and then, as best you can, to share His peace with your neighbors. But sometimes, that's easier said than done.

God offers peace that passes human understanding . . . and He wants you to make His peace your peace.

If you are a person with lots of obligations and plenty of responsibilities, it is simply a fact of life: You worry. From time to time, you worry about finances, safety, health, home, family, or about countless other concerns, some great and some small. Where is the best place to take your worries? Take them to God . . . and leave them there.

The Scottish preacher George McDonald observed, "It has been well said that no man ever sank under the burden of the day. It is when tomorrow's burden is added to the burden of today that the weight is more than a man can bear. Never load yourselves so, my friends. If you find yourselves so loaded, at least remember this: it is your own doing, not God's. He begs you to leave the future to Him."

Today, as a gift to yourself, to your family, and to your friends, claim the inner peace that is your spiritual birthright: the peace of Jesus Christ. Christ is standing at the door, waiting patiently for you to invite Him to reign over your heart. His eternal peace is offered freely. Claim it today.

STRENGTHENING YOUR FAITH

Does peace seem to be a distant promise? It is not. God's peace is available to you this very moment if you place absolute trust in Him. Elisabeth Elliot writes, "If my life is surrendered to God, all is well. Let me not grab it back, as though it were in peril in His hand but would be safer in mine!" Today, let go of your concerns by turning them over to God. Trust Him in the present moment, and accept His peace . . . in the present moment.

DAY 83

CONSIDER THE POSSIBILITIES

But Jesus looked at them and said, "With men this is impossible, but with God all things are possible."

Matthew 19:26 HCSB

All of us face difficult days. Sometimes even the most optimistic people can become discouraged, and you are no exception. If you find yourself enduring difficult circumstances, perhaps it's time for an extreme intellectual makeover—perhaps it's time to focus more on your strengths and opportunities, and less on the challenges that confront you. And one more thing: perhaps it's time to put a little more faith in God.

Don't invest large quantities of your life focusing on past misfortunes. On the road of life, regret is a dead end.

Every day, including this one, is brimming with possibilities. Every day is filled with opportunities to grow, to serve, and to share. But if you are entangled in a web of negativity, you may overlook the blessings that God has scattered along your path. So don't give in to pessimism, to doubt, or to cynicism. Instead, keep your eyes upon the possibilities, fix your heart upon the Creator, do your best, and let Him handle the rest.

FOOD FOR THOUGHT

When God is involved, anything can happen. Be open and stay that way. God has a beautiful way of bringing good vibrations out of broken chords.

Charles Swindoll

Life is a glorious opportunity.

Billy Graham

We are all faced with a series of great opportunities, brilliantly disguised as unsolvable problems. Unsolvable without God's wisdom, that is.

Charles Swindoll

With the right attitude and a willingness to pay the price, almost anyone can pursue nearly any opportunity and achieve it.

John Maxwell

A HEALTHY-CHOICE TIP

The cure for obesity is simple, but implementing that cure isn't. Weight loss requires lots of planning and lots of self-discipline. But with God's help, you're up to the task.

DAY 84

NEW BEGINNINGS

Then the One seated on the throne said, "Look! I am making everything new."

Revelation 21:5 HCSB

Each new day offers countless opportunities to serve God, to seek His will, and to obey His teachings. But each day also offers countless opportunities to stray from God's commandments and to wander far from His path.

Sometimes, we wander aimlessly in a wilderness of our own making, but God has better plans for us. And, whenever we ask Him to renew our strength and guide our steps, He does so.

Consider this day a new beginning. Consider it a fresh start, a renewed opportunity to serve your Creator with willing hands and a loving heart. Ask God to renew your sense of purpose as He guides your steps. Today is a glorious opportunity to serve God. Seize that opportunity while you can; tomorrow may indeed be too late.

If you're graduating into a new phase of life, be sure to make God your partner. If you do, He'll guide your steps, He'll help carry your burdens, and He'll help you focus on the things that really matter.

FOOD FOR THOUGHT

God is not running an antique shop! He is making all things new!

Vance Havner

The amazing thing about Jesus is that He doesn't just patch up our lives, He gives us a brand new sheet, a clean slate to start over, all new.

Gloria Gaither

Like a spring of pure water, God's peace in our hearts brings cleansing and refreshment to our minds and bodies.

Billy Graham

Whoever you are, whatever your condition or circumstance, whatever your past or problem, Jesus can restore you to wholeness.

Anne Graham Lotz

STRENGTHENING YOUR FAITH

How do you know if you can still keep growing as a Christian? Check your pulse. If it's still beating, then you can still keep growing.

DAY 85

THE RIGHT KIND OF EXAMPLE

You should be an example to the believers in speech, in conduct, in love, in faith, in purity.

1 Timothy 4:12 HCSB

Whether you know it or not, you're a role model. Your friends and family members watch your actions and make careful mental notes. Your obligation, of course, is to behave accordingly. After all, your words of instruction will never ring true unless you yourself are willing to follow them.

The words you choose to speak may have some impact on others, but not nearly as much impact as the life you choose to live.

What kind of example are you? Are you the kind of man whose life serves as a model of integrity and good judgment? Are you a believer whose behavior serves as a positive role model for others? Are you the kind of Christian whose actions, day in and day out, are based upon kindness, moderation, and a love for the Lord? If so, you are not only blessed by God, but you are also a powerful force for good in a world that desperately needs positive influences such as yours.

Corrie ten Boom advised, "Don't worry about what you do not understand. Worry about what you do understand in the Bible but do not live by." And Phillips Brooks advised, "Be such a man, and live such a life, that if every person were such as you, and every life a life like yours, this earth would be God's Paradise." That's sound advice because your family and friends are watching . . . and so, for that matter, is God.

FOOD FOR THOUGHT

We urgently need people who encourage and inspire us to move toward God and away from the world's enticing pleasures.

Jim Cymbala

In our faith we follow in someone's steps. In our faith we leave footprints to guide others. It's the principle of discipleship.

Max Lucado

A HEALTHY-CHOICE TIP

If you make healthy habits an important part of your own lifestyle, your close family members will, in all likelihood, follow your example.

DAY 86

KEEPING A PROPER PERSPECTIVE

All I'm doing right now, friends, is showing how these things pertain to Apollos and me so that you will learn restraint and not rush into making judgments without knowing all the facts. It is important to look at things from God's point of view. I would rather not see you inflating or deflating reputations based on mere hearsay.

1 Corinthians 4:6 MSG

For most of us, life is busy and complicated. Amid the rush and crush of the daily grind, it is easy to lose perspective . . . easy, but wrong. When the world seems to be spinning out of control, we can regain perspective by slowing ourselves down and then turning our thoughts and prayers toward God.

Keep life in perspective. Don't become unduly upset over the minor inconveniences of life, and don't worry too much about today's setbacks—they're temporary.

The familiar words of Psalm 46:10 remind us to "Be still, and know that I am God" (NKJV). When we do so, we are reminded of God's love (not to mention God's priorities), and we can then refocus our thoughts on the things that matter most. But, when we ignore the presence of our Creator—if we rush from place to place with scarcely a spare minute for God—we rob ourselves of His perspective, His peace, and His joy.

Do you carve out quiet moments each day to offer thanksgiving and praise to your Creator? You should. During these moments of stillness, you will often sense the love and wisdom of our Lord.

Today and every day, make time to be still before God. When you do, you can face the day's complications with the wisdom, the perspective, and the power that only He can provide.

FOOD FOR THOUGHT

What you see and hear depends a good deal on where you are standing; it also depends on what sort of person you are.

C. S. Lewis

A HEALTHY-CHOICE TIP

God's Word is full of advice about health, moderation, and sensible living. When you come across these passages, take them to heart and put them to use.

DAY 87

SAFETY FIRST

The sensible see danger and take cover; the foolish keep going and are punished.

Proverbs 27:12 HCSB

We live in a world that can be a dangerous place, especially for those who are inclined toward risky behaviors. Some risk takers are easy to spot: they jump out of little airplanes, scurry up tall mountains, or race very fast automobiles.

Most risk takers, however, are not so bold; instead, they take more subtle risks that endanger themselves, their friends, and their families. They drink and drive, or they smoke cigarettes, or they neglect to fasten their seatbelts, or they engage in countless other behaviors that, while not as glamorous as mountain climbing, are equally as dangerous.

Put the brakes on risky behaviors . . . before risky behaviors put the brakes on you.

This world holds enough hazards of its own without our adding to those risks by foolishly neglecting our own personal safety and the safety of those around us. So, the next time you're tempted to do something foolish, remember that the body you're putting at risk belongs not only to you, but also to God. And He hopes that you'll behave wisely.

FOOD FOR THOUGHT

Sometimes, being wise is nothing more than slowing down long enough to think about things before you do them.

Jim Gallery

If we neglect the Bible, we cannot expect to benefit from the wisdom and direction that result from knowing God's Word.

Vonette Bright

Wisdom is knowledge applied. Head knowledge is useless on the battlefield. Knowledge stamped on the heart makes one wise.

Beth Moore

The more wisdom enters our hearts, the more we will be able to trust our hearts in difficult situations.

John Eldredge

A HEALTHY-CHOICE TIP

Remember: life is God's gift to you—taking good care of yourself is your gift to God.

DAY 88

YOU DON'T HAVE TO BE PERFECT

To acquire wisdom is to love oneself; people who cherish understanding will prosper.

Proverbs 19:8 NLT

You don't have to be perfect to be wonderful. The difference between perfectionism and realistic expectations is the difference between a life of frustration and a life of contentment. Only one earthly being ever lived life to perfection, and He was the Son of God. The rest of us have fallen short of God's standard and need to be accepting of our own limitations as well as the limitations of others.

A perfectionist resists the truth that growing up in Christ is a process.

Susan Lenzkes

If you find yourself frustrated by the unrealistic demands of others (or by unrealistic pressures of the self-imposed variety) it's time to ask yourself who you're trying to impress, and why. Your first responsibility is to the Heavenly Father who created you and to the Son who saved you. Then, you bear a powerful responsibility to be true to yourself. And of course you owe debts of gratitude to friends and family members. But, when it comes to meeting society's unrealistic expectations, forget it! Those expectations aren't just unrealistic; they're detrimental to your spiritual health.

So, if you've become discouraged with your inability to be perfectly fit, remember that when you accepted Christ as your Savior, God accepted you for all eternity. Now, it's your turn to accept yourself. When you do, you'll feel a tremendous weight being lifted from your shoulders. After all, pleasing God is simply a matter of obeying His commandments and accepting His Son. But as for pleasing everybody else? That's impossible . . . so why even try?

STRENGTHENING YOUR FAITH

As you begin to work toward improved physical and emotional health, don't expect perfection. Of course you should work hard; of course you should be disciplined; of course you should do your best. But then, when you've given it your best effort, you should be accepting of yourself, imperfect though you may be. In heaven, we will know perfection. Here on earth, we have a few short years to wrestle with the challenges of imperfection. Let us accept these lives that God has given us—and these bodies which are ours for a brief time here on earth—with open, loving arms.

DAY 89

BEYOND THE SETBACKS

Peace, peace to you, and peace to him who helps you, for your God helps you.

1 Chronicles 12:18 HCSB

It's simply a fact of life: Not all of your health-related plans will succeed, and not all of your goals will be met. Life's occasional setbacks are simply the price that we must pay for our willingness to take risks as we follow our dreams. But even when we encounter bitter disappointments, we must never lose faith.

Remember that failure isn't permanent . . . unless you fail to get up. So pick yourself up, dust yourself off, and trust God. He will make it right.

Hebrews 10:36 advises, "Patient endurance is what you need now, so you will continue to do God's will. Then you will receive all that he has promised" (NLT). These words remind us that when we persevere, we will eventually receive the rewards which God has promised us. What's required is perseverance, not perfection.

When we face hardships, God stands ready to protect us. Our responsibility, of course, is to ask Him for protection. When we call upon Him in heartfelt prayer, He will answer—in His own time and according to His own plan—and He will do His part to heal us. We, of course, must do our part, too.

And, while we are waiting for God's plans to unfold and for His healing touch to restore us, we can be comforted in the knowledge that our Creator can overcome any obstacle, even if we cannot.

FOOD FOR THOUGHT

Success or failure can be pretty well predicted by the degree to which the heart is fully in it.

John Eldredge

Never imagine that you can be a loser by trusting in God.

C. H. Spurgeon

A HEALTHY-CHOICE TIP

If you're on a new health regimen, you may relapse back into your old, unhealthy habits. If so, don't waste time or energy beating yourself up. If you've "fallen off the wagon," simply pick yourself up, dust yourself off, and get back on it. God was with you when you were riding that wagon the first time, He was with you when you fell, and He'll welcome you back on the wagon when you're wise enough to climb back on.

DAY 90

GETTING ENOUGH REST?

Come to Me, all you who labor and are heavy laden, and I will give you rest. Take My yoke upon you and learn from Me, for I am gentle and lowly in heart, and you will find rest for your souls. For My yoke is easy and My burden is light.

Matthew 11:28-30 NKJV

Even the most inspired Christians can, from time to time, find themselves running on empty. The demands of daily life can drain us of our strength and rob us of the joy that is rightfully ours in Christ. When we find ourselves tired, discouraged, or worse, there is a source from which we can draw the power needed to recharge our spiritual batteries. That source is God.

God wants you to get enough rest. The world wants you to burn the candle at both ends. Trust God.

God intends that His children lead joyous lives filled with abundance and peace. But sometimes, abundance and peace seem very far away. It is then that we must turn to God for renewal, and when we do, He will restore us.

God expects us to work hard, but He also intends for us to rest. When we fail to take the rest that we need, we do a disservice to ourselves and to our families.

Is your spiritual battery running low? Is your energy on the wane? Are your emotions frayed? If so, it's time to turn your thoughts and your prayers to God. And when you're finished, it's time to rest.

FOOD FOR THOUGHT

Jesus gives us the ultimate rest, the confidence we need, to escape the frustration and chaos of the world around us.

Billy Graham

Jesus taught us by example to get out of the rat race and recharge our batteries.

Barbara Johnson

Life is strenuous. See that your clock does not run down.

Mrs. Charles E. Cowman

A HEALTHY-CHOICE TIP

You live in a world that tempts you to stay up late—very late. But too much late-night TV, combined with too little sleep, is a prescription for exhaustion, ill health, ill temper, or all three. So do yourself, your boss, and your loved ones a big favor. Arrange your TV schedule and your life so you get eight hours of sleep every night.

DAY 91

TOO FRIENDLY WITH THE WORLD?

Let no one deceive himself. If anyone among you seems to be wise in this age, let him become a fool that he may become wise. For the wisdom of this world is foolishness with God. For it is written, "He catches the wise in their own craftiness."

1 Corinthians 3:18–19 NKJV

We live in the world, but we should not worship it—yet at every turn, or so it seems, we are tempted to do otherwise. As Warren Wiersbe correctly observed, "Because the world is deceptive, it is dangerous."

> The world makes plenty of promises that it can't keep. God, on the other hand, keeps every single one of His promises.

The 21st-century world in which we live is a noisy, distracting place, a place that offers countless temptations and dangers. The world seems to cry, "Worship me with your time, your money, your energy, your thoughts, and your life!" But if we are wise, we won't fall prey to that temptation.

If you wish to build your character day-by-day, you must distance yourself, at least in part, from the temptations and distractions of modern-day society. But distancing yourself isn't easy, especially when so many societal forces are struggling to capture your attention, your participation, and your money.

C. S. Lewis said, "Aim at heaven and you will get earth thrown in; aim at earth and you will get neither." That's good advice. You're likely to hit what you aim at, so aim high . . . aim at heaven. When you do, you'll be strengthening your character as you improve every aspect of your life. And God will demonstrate His approval as He showers you with more spiritual blessings than you can count.

FOOD FOR THOUGHT

Our joy ends where love of the world begins.

C. H. Spurgeon

A HEALTHY-CHOICE TIP

Simply put, it's up to you to assume the ultimate responsibility for your health. So if you're fighting the battle of the bulge (the bulging waistline, that is), don't waste your time blaming the fast food industry—or anybody else, for that matter. It's your body and it's your responsibility to take care of it.

DAY 92

LIVING ON PURPOSE

He is the image of the invisible God, the firstborn over all creation; because by Him everything was created, in heaven and on earth, the visible and the invisible, whether thrones or dominions or rulers or authorities—all things have been created through Him and for Him.

Colossians 1:15-16 HCSB

"What did God put me here to do?" If you're like most people, you've asked yourself that question on many occasions. Perhaps you have pondered your future, uncertain of your plans, unsure of your next step. But even if you don't have a clear plan for the next step of your life's journey, you may rest assured that God does.

God has big things in store for you, but He may have quite a few lessons to teach you before you are fully prepared to do His will and fulfill His purpose.

God has a plan for the universe, and He has a plan for you. He understands that plan as thoroughly and completely as He knows you. If you seek God's will earnestly and prayerfully, He will make His plans known to you in His own time and in His own way.

Do you sincerely seek to discover God's purpose for your life? If so, you must first be willing to live in accordance with His commandments. You must also study

God's Word and be watchful for His signs. Finally, you should open yourself up to the Creator every day—beginning with this one—and you must have faith that He will soon reveal His plans to you.

Perhaps your vision of God's purpose for your life has been clouded by a wish list that you have expected God to dutifully fulfill. Perhaps, you have fervently hoped that God would create a world that unfolds according to your wishes, not His. If so, you have experienced more disappointment than satisfaction and more frustration than peace. A better strategy is to conform your will to God's (and not to struggle vainly in an attempt to conform His will to yours).

Sometimes, God's plans and purposes may seem unmistakably clear to you. If so, push ahead. But other times, He may lead you through the wilderness before He directs you to the Promised Land. So be patient and keep seeking His will for your life. When you do, you'll be amazed at the marvelous things that an all-powerful, all-knowing God can do.

A HEALTHY-CHOICE TIP

Don't worship food. Honor the body that God gave you by eating sensible portions of sensible foods.

DAY 93

BE STILL

Be still, and know that I am God.

Psalm 46:10 NKJV

We live in a noisy world, a world filled with distractions, frustrations, obligations, and complications. But we must not allow our clamorous world to separate us from God's peace. Instead, we must "be still" so that we might sense the presence of God.

If we are to maintain righteous minds and compassionate hearts, we must take time each day for prayer and for meditation. We must make ourselves still in the presence of our Creator. We must quiet our minds and our hearts so that we might sense God's love, God's will, and God's Son.

Has the busy pace of life robbed you of the peace that might otherwise be yours through Jesus Christ? If so, it's time to reorder your priorities. Nothing is more important than the time you spend with your Savior. So be still and claim the inner peace that is your spiritual birthright: the peace of Jesus Christ. It is offered freely; it has been paid for in full; it is yours for the asking. So ask. And then share.

Spend a few moments each day in silence. You owe it to your Creator . . . and to yourself.

FOOD FOR THOUGHT

Growth takes place in quietness, in hidden ways, in silence and solitude. The process is not accessible to observation.

Eugene Peterson

As we find that it is not easy to persevere in this being "alone with God," we begin to realize that it is because we are not "wholly for God." God has a right to demand that He should have us completely for Himself.

Andrew Murray

A quiet time is a basic ingredient in a maturing relationship with God.

Charles Stanley

When we are in the presence of God, removed from distractions, we are able to hear him more clearly, and a secure environment has been established for the young and broken places in our hearts to surface.

John Eldredge

A HEALTHY-CHOICE TIP

It's simple: When you're treating your body like a temple, you're obeying God; when you're abusing your body, you're disobeying Him.

DAY 94

REMEMBER THE SABBATH

Remember the Sabbath day, to keep it holy.

Exodus 20:8 NKJV

When God gave Moses the Ten Commandments, it became perfectly clear that our Heavenly Father intends for us to make the Sabbath a holy day, a day for worship, for contemplation, for fellowship, and for rest. Yet we live in a seven-day-a-week world, a world that all too often treats Sunday as a regular workday.

One way to strengthen your faith is by giving God at least one day each week. If you carve out the time for a day of worship and praise, you'll be amazed at the impact it will have on the rest of your week. But if you fail to honor God's day, if you treat the Sabbath as a day to work or a day to party, you'll miss out on a harvest of blessings that is only available one day each week.

The Sabbath is unlike the other six days of the week, and it's up to you to treat it that way.

How does your family observe the Lord's day? When church is over, do you treat Sunday like any other day of the week? If so, it's time to think long and hard about your family's schedule and your family's priorities. And if you've been treating Sunday as just another day, it's time to break that habit.

FOOD FOR THOUGHT

Jesus gives us the ultimate rest, the confidence we need, to escape the frustration and chaos of the world around us.

Billy Graham

It is what Jesus is, not what we are, that gives rest to the soul. If we really want to overcome Satan and have peace with God, we must "fix our eyes on Jesus." Let his death, his suffering, his glories, and his intercession be fresh on your mind.

C. H. Spurgeon

One reason so much American Christianity is a mile wide and an inch deep is that Christians are simply tired. Sometimes you need to kick back and rest for Jesus' sake.

Dennis Swanberg

STRENGTHENING YOUR FAITH

Working seven days a week may impress your boss . . . but it isn't the way God intends for you to live your life. You live in a world that doesn't often honor the Sabbath, but God wants you to treat the Sabbath as a day of rest, no exceptions. So next Sunday, do yourself and your family a favor: take God at His word by making the Sabbath a special day for you and your family.

DAY 95

VALUE-BASED DECISIONS

We encouraged, comforted, and implored each one of you to walk worthy of God, who calls you into His own kingdom and glory.

1 Thessalonians 2:12 HCSB

Society seeks to impose its set of values upon you, however these values are often contrary to God's Word (and thus contrary to your own best interests). The world makes promises that it simply cannot fulfill. It promises happiness, contentment, prosperity, and abundance. But genuine abundance is not a by-product of possessions or status; it is a by-product of your thoughts, your actions, and your relationship with God. The world's promises are incomplete and deceptive; God's promises are unfailing. Your challenge, then, is to build your value system upon the firm foundation of God's promises . . . nothing else will suffice.

You can have the values that the world holds dear, or you can have the values that God holds dear, but you can't have both.

As a citizen of the 21st century, you live in a world that is filled with countless opportunities to make major mistakes. The world seems to cry, "Worship me with your time, your money, your energy, and your thoughts!" But God commands otherwise: He commands you to worship Him and Him alone; everything else must be secondary.

So, when you're faced with a difficult choice or a powerful temptation, seek God's counsel and trust the counsel that He gives. Invite God into your heart and live according to His commandments. Study His Word and talk to Him often. When you do, you will share in the abundance and peace that only God can give.

FOOD FOR THOUGHT

As the first community to which a person is attached and the first authority under which a person learns to live, the family establishes society's most basic values.

Charles Colson

Whether you have twenty years left, ten years, one year, one month, one day, or just one hour, there is something very important God wants you to do that can add to His kingdom and your blessing.

Bill Bright

A HEALTHY-CHOICE TIP

If you place a high value on the body God has given you, then place high importance on the foods you use to fuel it.

DAY 96

LIFETIME LEARNING

The wise person makes learning a joy; fools spout only foolishness.

Proverbs 15:2 NLT

When it comes to learning life's lessons, we can either do things the easy way or the hard way. The easy way can be summed up as follows: when God teaches us a lesson, we learn it . . . the first time! Unfortunately, too many of us—both parents and children alike—learn much more slowly than that.

God still has important lessons to teach you. Your task is to be open to His instruction.

When we resist God's instruction, He continues to teach, whether we like it or not. And if we keep making the same old mistakes, God responds by rewarding us with the same old results.

Our challenge, then, is to discern God's lessons from the experiences of everyday life. Hopefully, we learn those lessons sooner rather than later because the sooner we do, the sooner He can move on to the next lesson and the next, and the next . . .

FOOD FOR THOUGHT

True learning can take place at every age of life, and it doesn't have to be in the curriculum plan.

Suzanne Dale Ezell

While chastening is always difficult, if we look to God for the lesson we should learn, we will see spiritual fruit.

Vonette Bright

The wonderful thing about God's schoolroom is that we get to grade our own papers. You see, He doesn't test us so He can learn how well we're doing. He tests us so we can discover how well we're doing.

Charles Swindoll

STRENGTHENING YOUR FAITH

Today is your classroom: what will you learn? Will you use today's experiences as tools for personal, spiritual, and physical improvement, or will you ignore the lessons that life and God are trying to teach you? Will you carefully study God's Word, and will you apply His teachings to the experiences of everyday life? The events of today have much to teach. You have much to learn. May you live—and learn—accordingly.

DAY 97

PROBLEM-SOLVING MADE SIMPLE

Many adversities come to the one who is righteous, but the Lord delivers him from them all.

Psalm 34:19 HCSB

Life is an adventure in problem-solving. The question is not whether we will encounter problems; the real question is how we will choose to address them. When it comes to solving the problems of everyday living, we often know precisely what needs to be done, but we may be slow in doing it—especially if what needs to be done is difficult. So we put off till tomorrow what should be done today.

As a person living here in the 21st century, you have your own set of challenges. As you face those challenges, you may be comforted by this fact: Trouble, of every kind, is temporary. Yet God's grace is eternal. And worries, of every kind, are temporary. But God's love is everlasting. The troubles that concern you will pass. God remains. And for every problem, God has a solution.

Remember that "this, too, will pass," but whatever "it" is will pass more quickly if you spend more time solving your problems and less time fretting about them.

The words of Psalm 34 remind us that the Lord solves problems for "people who do what is right." And usually, doing "what is right" means doing the uncomfortable work of confronting our problems sooner rather than later. So with no further ado, let the problem-solving begin . . . right now.

FOOD FOR THOUGHT

We are all faced with a series of great opportunities, brilliantly disguised as unsolvable problems. Unsolvable without God's wisdom, that is.

Charles Swindoll

Life will be made or broken at the place where we meet and deal with obstacles.

E. Stanley Jones

Each problem is a God-appointed instructor.

Charles Swindoll

A HEALTHY-CHOICE TIP

As exercise increases, stress usually decreases. So, if you want less stress in your life, you should exercise more frequently.

DAY 98

FITNESS IS A FORM OF WORSHIP

Worship the Lord your God and . . . serve Him only.

Matthew 4:10 HCSB

What does worship have to do with fitness? That depends on how you define worship. If you consider worship to be a "Sunday-only" activity, an activity that occurs only inside the four walls of your local church, then fitness and worship may seem totally unrelated. But, if you view worship as an activity that impacts every facet of your life—if you consider worship to be something far more than a "one-day-a week" obligation—then you understand that every aspect of your life is a form of worship. And that includes keeping your body physically fit.

When you worship God with a sincere heart, He will guide your steps and bless your life.

Every day provides opportunities to put God where He belongs: at the center of our lives. When we do so, we worship not just with our words, but also with our deeds. And one way that we can honor our Heavenly Father is by treating our bodies with care and respect.

The Bible makes it clear: "Your body is the temple of the Holy Spirit" (1 Corinthians 6:19 NLT). Treat it that way. And consider your fitness regimen to be one way—a very important way—of worshipping God.

FOOD FOR THOUGHT

It's the definition of worship: A hungry heart finding the Father's feast. A searching soul finding the Father's face. A wandering pilgrim spotting the Father's house. Finding God. Finding God seeking us. This is worship. This is a worshiper.

Max Lucado

Spiritual worship is focusing all we are on all He is.

Beth Moore

There is no division into sacred and secular; it is all one great, glorious life.

Oswald Chambers

God asks that we worship Him with our concentrated minds as well as with our wills and emotions. A divided and scattered mind is not effective.

Catherine Marshall

A HEALTHY-CHOICE TIP

If you're in reasonably good shape, a nice healthy walk can be a great substitute for a big sit-down meal. So don't underestimate the benefits of a good walk. It's a great way to burn a few calories, to get some fresh air, and to improve your life.

DAY 99

YOUR PHYSICAL AND SPIRITUAL FITNESS: WHO'S IN CHARGE?

But seek ye first the kingdom of God, and his righteousness; and all these things shall be added unto you.

Matthew 6:33 KJV

One of the surest ways to improve your health and your life—and the best way—is to do it with God as your partner. When you put God first in every aspect of your life, you'll be comforted by the knowledge that His wisdom is the ultimate wisdom and that His plans are the right plans for you. When you put God first, your outlook will change, your priorities will change, your behaviors will change, and your health will change. When you put Him first, you'll experience the genuine peace and lasting comfort that only He can give.

God deserves first place in your life . . . and you deserve the experience of putting Him there.

In the book of Exodus, God instructs us to place no gods before Him (20:3). Does God rule your heart? Make certain that the honest answer to this question is a resounding yes. And then prepare yourself for the cascade of spiritual and emotional blessings that are sure to follow.

FOOD FOR THOUGHT

The LORD is my strength and my song; he has become my victory. He is my God, and I will praise him.

Exodus 15:2 NLT

Love the Lord your God with all your heart, with all your soul, and with all your strength.

Deuteronomy 6:5 HCSB

Make God's will the focus of your life day by day. If you seek to please Him and Him alone, you'll find yourself satisfied with life.

Kay Arthur

Jesus Christ is the first and last, author and finisher, beginning and end, alpha and omega, and by Him all other things hold together. He must be first or nothing. God never comes next!

Vance Havner

STRENGTHENING YOUR FAITH

God has a plan for the world and for you. When you discover His plan for your life—and when you follow in the footsteps of His Son—you will be rewarded. The place where God is leading you is the place where you must go.

DAY 100

GIVE HIM YOUR HEART

For God so loved the world that He gave His only begotten Son, that whoever believes in Him should not perish but have everlasting life.

John 3:16 NKJV

Your decision to allow Christ to reign over your heart is the pivotal decision of your life. It is a decision that you cannot ignore. It is a decision that is yours and yours alone.

God's love for you is deeper and more profound than you can imagine. God's love for you is so great that He sent His only Son to this earth to die for your sins and to offer you the priceless gift of eternal life. Now, you must decide whether or not to accept God's gift. Will you ignore it or embrace it? Will you return it or neglect it? Will you accept Christ's love and build a lifelong relationship with Him, or will you turn away from Him and take a different path?

The ultimate choice for you is the choice to invite God's Son into your heart. Choose wisely . . . and immediately.

Accept God's gift now: allow His Son to preside over your heart, your thoughts, and your life, starting this very instant.

FOOD FOR THOUGHT

Jesus is the personal approach from the unseen God coming so near that he becomes inescapable. You don't have to find him—you just have to consent to be found.

E. Stanley Jones

Someday you will read in the papers that Moody is dead. Don't you believe a word of it. At that moment I shall be more alive than I am now. I was born of the flesh in 1837, I was born of the spirit in 1855. That which is born of the flesh may die. That which is born of the Spirit shall live forever.

D. L. Moody

Once a man is united to God, how could he not live forever? Once a man is separated from God, what can he do but wither and die?

C. S. Lewis

STRENGTHENING YOUR FAITH

If you've already accepted Christ into your heart, congratulations! If you haven't, the appropriate moment to do so is this one.

MORE FROM GOD'S WORD

Verses by Topic

FAITH

If you do not stand firm in your faith, then you will not stand at all.

Isaiah 7:9 HCSB

Be alert, stand firm in the faith, be brave and strong.

1 Corinthians 16:13 HCSB

For we walk by faith, not by sight.

2 Corinthians 5:7 HCSB

Now faith is the reality of what is hoped for, the proof of what is not seen.

Hebrews 11:1 HCSB

Now without faith it is impossible to please God, for the one who draws near to Him must believe that He exists and rewards those who seek Him.

Hebrews 11:6 HCSB

GOD'S LOVE

For God loved the world in this way: He gave His only Son, so that everyone who believes in Him will not perish but have eternal life.

John 3:16 HCSB

For the Lord is good, and His love is eternal; His faithfulness endures through all generations.

Psalm 100:5 HCSB

The one who has My commandments and keeps them is the one who loves Me. And the one who loves Me will be loved by My Father. I also will love him and will reveal Myself to him.

John 14:21 HCSB

We love Him because He first loved us.

1 John 4:19 NKJV

Draw near to God, and He will draw near to you.

James 4:8 HCSB

WISDOM

Therefore, everyone who hears these words of Mine and acts on them will be like a sensible man who built his house on the rock. The rain fell, the rivers rose, and the winds blew and pounded that house. Yet it didn't collapse, because its foundation was on the rock.

Matthew 7:24–25 HCSB

But from Him you are in Christ Jesus, who for us became wisdom from God, as well as righteousness, sanctification, and redemption.

1 *Corinthians* 1:30 HCSB

For God has not given us a spirit of fearfulness, but one of power, love, and sound judgment.

2 *Timothy* 1:7 HCSB

Now if any of you lacks wisdom, he should ask God, who gives to all generously and without criticizing, and it will be given to him.

James 1:5 HCSB

THE SIMPLE LIFE

A simple life in the Fear-of-God is better than a rich life with a ton of headaches.

Proverbs 15:16 MSG

Do not love the world or the things in the world. If anyone loves the world, the love of the Father is not in him.

1 John 2:15 NKJV

We brought nothing into the world, so we can take nothing out. But, if we have food and clothes, we will be satisfied with that.

1 Timothy 6:7-8 NCV

So think clearly and exercise self-control. Look forward to the special blessings that will come to you at the return of Jesus Christ.

1 Peter 1:13 NLT

For the grace of God has been revealed, bringing salvation to all people. And we are instructed to turn from godless living and sinful pleasures. We should live in this evil world with self-control, right conduct, and devotion to God.

Titus 2:11-12 NLT

RIGHTEOUSNESS

The righteous one will live by his faith.

Habakkuk 2:4 HCSB

And the world is passing away, and the lust of it; but he who does the will of God abides forever.

1 John 2:17 NKJV

Because the eyes of the Lord are on the righteous and His ears are open to their request. But the face of the Lord is against those who do evil.

1 Peter 3:12 HCSB

Flee from youthful passions, and pursue righteousness, faith, love, and peace, along with those who call on the Lord from a pure heart.

2 Timothy 2:22 HCSB

And now, Israel, what does the Lord your God ask of you except to fear the Lord your God by walking in all His ways, to love Him, and to worship the Lord your God with all your heart and all your soul?

Deuteronomy 10:12 HCSB

YOUR PRIORITIES

Don't abandon wisdom, and she will watch over you; love her, and she will guard you.

Proverbs 4:6 HCSB

And I pray this: that your love will keep on growing in knowledge and every kind of discernment, so that you can determine what really matters and can be pure and blameless in the day of Christ.

Philippians 1:9 HCSB

So teach us to number our days, that we may gain a heart of wisdom.

Psalm 90:12 NKJV

For where your treasure is, there your heart will be also.

Luke 12:34 HCSB

He said to them all, "If anyone desires to come after Me, let him deny himself, and take up his cross daily, and follow Me. For whoever desires to save his life will lose it, but whoever loses his life for My sake will save it."

Luke 9:23-24 NKJV

ASKING FOR GOD'S HELP

If you remain in Me and My words remain in you, ask whatever you want and it will be done for you.

John 15:7 HCSB

What father among you, if his son asks for a fish, will, instead of a fish, give him a snake? Or if he asks for an egg, will give him a scorpion? If you then, who are evil, know how to give good gifts to your children, how much more will the heavenly Father give the Holy Spirit to those who ask Him?

Luke 11:11-13 HCSB

Don't worry about anything, but in everything, through prayer and petition with thanksgiving, let your requests be made known to God.

Philippians 4:6 HCSB

You do not have because you do not ask.

James 4:2 HCSB

For the Lord gives wisdom; from His mouth come knowledge and understanding.

Proverbs 2:6 NKJV

GOD'S STRENGTH

Be of good courage, and let us be strong for our people and for the cities of our God. And may the Lord do what is good in His sight.

1 Chronicles 19:13 NKJV

Do you not know? Have you not heard? The Everlasting God, the LORD, the Creator of the ends of the earth does not become weary or tired. His understanding is inscrutable. He gives strength to the weary, and to him who lacks might He increases power. Though youths grow weary and tired, and vigorous young men stumble badly, yet those who wait for the LORD will gain new strength; they will mount up with wings like eagles, they will run and not get tired, they will walk and not become weary.

Isaiah 40:28–31 NASB

He said unto me, My grace is sufficient for thee: for my strength is made perfect in weakness.

2 Corinthians 12:9 KJV

The LORD is my strength and my song....

Exodus 15:2 NIV

LIFE

I urge you now to live the life to which God called you.

Ephesians 4:1 NKJV

Shout triumphantly to the Lord, all the earth. Serve the Lord with gladness; come before Him with joyful songs.

Psalm 100:1-2 HCSB

Rejoice in the Lord always. Again I will say, rejoice!

Philippians 4:4 NKJV

Jesus told him, "I am the way, the truth, and the life. No one comes to the Father except through Me."

John 14:6 HCSB

He who follows righteousness and mercy finds life, righteousness and honor.

Proverbs 21:21 NKJV

LIFETIME LEARNING

A wise person pays attention to correction that will improve his life.

Proverbs 15:31 ICB

Remember what you are taught, and listen carefully to words of knowledge.

Proverbs 23:12 NCV

The fear of the Lord is the beginning of knowledge, but fools despise wisdom and discipline.

Proverbs 1:7 NIV

The knowledge of the secrets of the kingdom of heaven has been given to you....

Matthew 13:11 NIV

It is not good to have zeal without knowledge, nor to be hasty and miss the way.

Proverbs 19:2 NIV

SILENCE

Be still, and know that I am God.

Psalm 46:10 NKJV

Be silent before the Lord and wait expectantly for Him.

Psalm 37:7 HCSB

In quietness and confidence shall be your strength.

Isaiah 30:15 NKJV

I am not alone, because the Father is with Me.

John 16:32 HCSB

Draw near to God, and He will draw near to you.

James 4:8 HCSB

VALUES

God's Way is not a matter of mere talk; it's an empowered life.

1 Corinthians 4:20 MSG

Walk in a manner worthy of the God who calls you into His own kingdom and glory.

1 Thessalonians 2:12 NASB

Therefore, since we have this ministry, as we have received mercy, we do not give up. Instead, we have renounced shameful secret things, not walking in deceit or distorting God's message, but in God's sight we commend ourselves to every person's conscience by an open display of the truth.

2 Corinthians 4:1-2 HCSB

We must not become tired of doing good. We will receive our harvest of eternal life at the right time if we do not give up.

Galatians 6:9 NCV

Blessed are those who hunger and thirst for righteousness, because they will be filled.

Matthew 5:6 HCSB

DOING THE RIGHT THING

The righteous one will live by his faith.

Habakkuk 2:4 HCSB

And the world is passing away, and the lust of it; but he who does the will of God abides forever.

1 John 2:17 NKJV

Because the eyes of the Lord are on the righteous and His ears are open to their request. But the face of the Lord is against those who do evil.

1 Peter 3:12 HCSB

Flee from youthful passions, and pursue righteousness, faith, love, and peace, along with those who call on the Lord from a pure heart.

2 Timothy 2:22 HCSB

Sow righteousness for yourselves and reap faithful love; break up your untilled ground. It is time to seek the Lord until He comes and sends righteousness on you like the rain.

Hosea 10:12 HCSB

PEACE

And the peace of God, which surpasses every thought, will guard your hearts and your minds in Christ Jesus. Finally brothers, whatever is true, whatever is honorable, whatever is just, whatever is pure, whatever is lovely, whatever is commendable—if there is any moral excellence and if there is any praise—dwell on these things.

Philippians 4:7-8 HCSB

Abundant peace belongs to those who love Your instruction; nothing makes them stumble.

Psalm 119:165 HCSB

You will keep in perfect peace him whose mind is steadfast, because he trusts in you.

Isaiah 26:3 NIV

I have told you these things so that in Me you may have peace. In the world you have suffering. But take courage! I have conquered the world.

John 16:33 HCSB

GOD'S GRACE

But God, who is abundant in mercy, because of His great love that He had for us, made us alive with the Messiah even though we were dead in trespasses. By grace you are saved!

Ephesians 2:4-5 HCSB

My grace is sufficient for you, for My strength is made perfect in weakness.

2 Corinthians 12:9 NKJV

And we have seen and testify that the Father has sent the Son as Savior of the world.

1 John 4:14 NKJV

For by grace you are saved through faith, and this is not from yourselves; it is God's gift—not from works, so that no one can boast.

Ephesians 2:8-9 HCSB

In Him we have redemption through His blood, the forgiveness of our trespasses, according to the riches of His grace that He lavished on us with all wisdom and understanding.

Ephesians 1:7-8 HCSB

THE DIRECTION OF YOUR THOUGHTS

Set your minds on what is above, not on what is on the earth.

Colossians 3:2 HCSB

Brothers, don't be childish in your thinking, but be infants in evil and adult in your thinking.

1 Corinthians 14:20 HCSB

Guard your heart above all else, for it is the source of life.

Proverbs 4:23 HCSB

May the words of my mouth and the meditation of my heart be acceptable to You, Lord, my rock and my Redeemer.

Psalm 19:14 HCSB

Commit your works to the Lord, and your thoughts will be established.

Proverbs 16:3 NKJV

TRUSTING GOD

Lord, I turn my hope to You. My God, I trust in You. Do not let me be disgraced; do not let my enemies gloat over me.

Psalm 25:1-2 HCSB

He granted their request because they trusted in Him.

1 Chronicles 5:20 HCSB

The one who understands a matter finds success, and the one who trusts in the Lord will be happy.

Proverbs 16:20 HCSB

The fear of man is a snare, but the one who trusts in the Lord is protected.

Proverbs 29:25 HCSB

Those who trust in the Lord are like Mount Zion. It cannot be shaken; it remains forever.

Psalm 125:1 HCSB

GOD'S FAITHFULNESS

I will sing of the tender mercies of the Lord forever! Young and old will hear of your faithfulness. Your unfailing love will last forever. Your faithfulness is as enduring as the heavens.

Psalm 89:1-2 NLT

God is faithful, by whom you were called into the fellowship of His Son, Jesus Christ our Lord.

1 Corinthians 1:9 NKJV

Because of the LORD'S great love we are not consumed, for his compassions never fail. They are new every morning; great is your faithfulness.

Lamentations 3:22-23 NIV

Blessed is he whose help is the God of Jacob, whose hope is in the LORD his God, the Maker of heaven and earth, the sea, and everything in them—the LORD, who remains faithful forever.

Psalm 146:5-6 NIV

BIBLE STUDY

All Scripture is inspired by God and is profitable for teaching, for rebuking, for correcting, for training in righteousness, so that the man of God may be complete, equipped for every good work.

2 Timothy 3:16-17 HCSB

Man shall not live by bread alone, but by every word that proceeds from the mouth of God.

Matthew 4:4 NKJV

Heaven and earth will pass away, but My words will never pass away.

Matthew 24:35 HCSB

For the word of God is living and effective and sharper than any two-edged sword, penetrating as far as to divide soul, spirit, joints, and marrow; it is a judge of the ideas and thoughts of the heart.

Hebrews 4:12 HCSB

PRAISE AND THANKSGIVING

It is good to give thanks to the Lord, and to sing praises to Your name, O Most High.

Psalm 92:1 NKJV

And let the peace of the Messiah, to which you were also called in one body, control your hearts. Be thankful.

Colossians 3:15 HCSB

Therefore as you have received Christ Jesus the Lord, walk in Him, rooted and built up in Him and established in the faith, just as you were taught, and overflowing with thankfulness.

Colossians 2:6-7 HCSB

In everything give thanks; for this is the will of God in Christ Jesus for you.

1 Thessalonians 5:18 NKJV

So that at the name of Jesus every knee should bow—of those who are in heaven and on earth and under the earth—and every tongue should confess that Jesus Christ is Lord, to the glory of God the Father.

Philippians 2:10-11 HCSB

JOY

Rejoice in the Lord always. I will say it again: Rejoice!

Philippians 4:4 HCSB

You will show me the way of life, granting me the joy of your presence and the pleasures of living with you forever.

Psalm 16:11 NLT

David and the whole house of Israel were celebrating before the Lord.

2 Samuel 6:5 HCSB

Their sorrow was turned into rejoicing and their mourning into a holiday. They were to be days of feasting, rejoicing, and of sending gifts to one another and the poor.

Esther 9:22 HCSB

At the dedication of the wall of Jerusalem, they sent for the Levites wherever they lived and brought them to Jerusalem to celebrate the joyous dedication with thanksgiving and singing accompanied by cymbals, harps, and lyres.

Nehemiah 12:27 HCSB

ABUNDANCE

I have come that they may have life, and that they may have it more abundantly.

John 10:10 NKJV

And God is able to make every grace overflow to you, so that in every way, always having everything you need, you may excel in every good work.

2 Corinthians 9:8 HCSB

Until now you have asked for nothing in My name. Ask and you will receive, that your joy may be complete.

John 16:24 HCSB

Come to terms with God and be at peace; in this way good will come to you.

Job 22:21 HCSB

My cup runs over. Surely goodness and mercy shall follow me all the days of my life; and I will dwell in the house of the Lord forever.

Psalm 23:5-6 NKJV

ANXIETY

Therefore don't worry about tomorrow, because tomorrow will worry about itself. Each day has enough trouble of its own.

Matthew 6:34 HCSB

Anxiety in a man's heart weighs it down, but a good word cheers it up.

Proverbs 12:25 HCSB

Why am I so depressed? Why this turmoil within me? Put your hope in God, for I will still praise Him, my Savior and my God.

Psalm 42:11 HCSB

In the multitude of my anxieties within me, Your comforts delight my soul.

Psalm 94:19 NKJV

Be anxious for nothing, but in everything by prayer and supplication, with thanksgiving, let your requests be made known to God.

Philippians 4:6 NKJV

CONFIDENCE

God also bound himself with an oath, so that those who received the promise could be perfectly sure that he would never change his mind. So God has given us both his promise and his oath. These two things are unchangeable because it is impossible for God to lie. Therefore, we who have fled to him for refuge can take new courage, for we can hold on to his promise with confidence.

Hebrews 6:17-18 NLT

The result of righteousness will be peace; the effect of righteousness will be quiet confidence forever.

Isaiah 32:17 HCSB

I've told you all this so that trusting me, you will be unshakable and assured, deeply at peace. In this godless world you will continue to experience difficulties. But take heart! I've conquered the world.

John 16:33 MSG

You are my hope; O Lord GOD, You are my confidence.

Psalm 71:5 NASB

ENCOURAGING OTHERS

I want their hearts to be encouraged and joined together in love, so that they may have all the riches of assured understanding, and have the knowledge of God's mystery—Christ.

Colossians 2:2 HCSB

And let us be concerned about one another in order to promote love and good works.

Hebrews 10:24 HCSB

Carry one another's burdens; in this way you will fulfill the law of Christ.

Galatians 6:2 HCSB

But encourage each other daily, while it is still called today, so that none of you is hardened by sin's deception.

Hebrews 3:13 HCSB

Iron sharpens iron, and one man sharpens another.

Proverbs 27:17 HCSB

GOD'S COMMANDMENTS

If only you had paid attention to My commands. Then your peace would have been like a river, and your righteousness like the waves of the sea.

Isaiah 48:18 HCSB

This is how we are sure that we have come to know Him: by keeping His commands.

1 John 2:3 HCSB

For this is the love of God, that we keep His commandments. And His commandments are not burdensome.

1 John 5:3 NKJV

Follow the whole instruction the Lord your God has commanded you, so that you may live, prosper, and have a long life in the land you will possess.

Deuteronomy 5:33 HCSB

He who has My commandments and keeps them, it is he who loves Me. And he who loves Me will be loved by My Father, and I will love him and manifest Myself to him.

John 14:21 NKJV

GOD'S PRESENCE

Draw near to God, and He will draw near to you.

James 4:8 HCSB

You will seek Me and find Me when you search for Me with all your heart.

Jeremiah 29:13 HCSB

The Lord is near all who call out to Him, all who call out to Him with integrity. He fulfills the desires of those who fear Him; He hears their cry for help and saves them.

Psalm 145:18-19 HCSB

Surely goodness and mercy shall follow me all the days of my life: and I will dwell in the house of the Lord for ever.

Psalm 23:6 KJV

I am not alone, because the Father is with Me.

John 16:32 HCSB

GOD'S TIMING

He said to them, "It is not for you to know times or periods that the Father has set by His own authority."

Acts 1:7 HCSB

Therefore the Lord is waiting to show you mercy, and is rising up to show you compassion, for the Lord is a just God. Happy are all who wait patiently for Him.

Isaiah 30:18 HCSB

But those who wait on the LORD shall renew their strength; they shall mount up with wings like eagles, they shall run and not be weary, they shall walk and not faint.

Isaiah 40:31 NKJV

To everything there is a season, a time for every purpose under heaven.

Ecclesiastes 3:1 NKJV

I waited patiently for the LORD; and He inclined to me, and heard my cry.

Psalm 40:1 NKJV

JESUS

The next day John saw Jesus coming toward him and said, "Here is the Lamb of God, who takes away the sin of the world!"

John 1:29 HCSB

I am the door. If anyone enters by Me, he will be saved.

John 10:9 NKJV

I have come as a light into the world, so that everyone who believes in Me would not remain in darkness.

John 12:46 HCSB

I am the true vine, and My Father is the vineyard keeper. Every branch in Me that does not produce fruit He removes, and He prunes every branch that produces fruit so that it will produce more fruit.

John 15:1-2 HCSB

But we do see Jesus—made lower than the angels for a short time so that by God's grace He might taste death for everyone—crowned with glory and honor because of the suffering of death.

Hebrews 2:9 HCSB